All About Deer Hunting in America

ALL ABOUT
DEER
HUNTING
IN AMERICA

Edited by ROBERT ELMAN

WINCHESTER PRESS   NEW YORK

Library of Congress Cataloging in Publication Data
Main entry under title:

All about deer hunting in America.

    Includes index.
    1. Deer hunting—United States. 2. Hunting—
United States. I. Elman, Robert.
SK301.A44   799.2'77'357   76-12560
ISBN 0-87691-176-9

WINCHESTER is a Trademark of Olin Corporation used by
Winchester Press, Inc. under authority and control of
the Trademark Proprietor.

Published by Winchester Press
205 East 42nd Street
New York, N.Y. 10017
Printed in the U.S.A.

To Ellen, John, and Paul—the Schwartz family of hunters—
and their friends and mine who have warmed
themselves before my fire and traded ideas about the likeliest
ways to add another set of antlers to the cabin wall.

CONTENTS

Introduction

A typewriter is not exactly the most common piece of equipment in a deer camp, but a writer or editor is apt to have his tools with him almost anywhere. I keep a typewriter at a permanent and favorite deer camp, my hunting cabin in the Poconos, and that's where I am as I write this introduction to a book I've thoroughly enjoyed compiling and editing. Just now, glancing through the window, I noticed the heavy iron look of the sky above the gray ridge. I think it's going to snow—I hope so because I plan to still-hunt tomorrow morning. And I know for certain that it's cold out there, because I've been in the woods most of the day and the only reason I came in before sundown was to get this introduction written.

I didn't get my deer today, but there's venison in the freezer back home since I had better luck (or more probably better deer sense) on opening day in another state. Besides, tomorrow is another day and I'll be happy to keep on trying. But first, here and now, I have to think hard about what needs to be said in this introduction. I'm very pleased with this book; and I'm also very pleased about the current deer population, not only here in the Pennsylvania woods but in Texas, Alabama, Missouri, the Dakotas, Colorado—in fact, throughout most regions of the country. Yet I'm not entirely pleased with today's deer-hunting trends (or with today's deer hunters) and as I write this introduction I'm feeling what second-rate novelists used to call mixed emotions. I have good news and not such good news. First the good news, both about this book but also about America's deer.

I've just finished editing the last chapter—Don McKnight's intriguing account of the Sitka blacktail, a deer of the Far North and therefore a deer known to relatively few American hunters, but nonetheless a game animal very much worth knowing. And I've looked back over the other 17 chapters, written by nationally respected authorities and dealing with all of the country's varieties of mule deer and whitetails and all of the most successful ways to hunt them. Reading all this deer-hunting lore by Jim Carmichel, Byron Dalrymple, Norm Strung, Russ Tinsley, "Joe" Bauer, Tom Brakefield, and others with comparable credentials, I feel a surge of

9

not very modest pride in my editorship. I recruited top experts and it feels good, upon finishing a job, to know it's a job well done.

Use the book wisely and it will make you a better deer hunter. No book (regardless of the jacket blurbs I've seen on a few) can guarantee venison in the freezer this season or next, but this one can improve your chances by a big margin. Between the covers of this volume, the contributors and I have compiled the tested techniques and secrets of this continent's experts, covering every region, every technique, every type of sporting arm, and every huntable variety of whitetail and mule deer. You'll notice a regional emphasis, and therein lies a major reason for recruiting experts from all over. If you think whitetails are whitetails, for instance, and are hunted pretty much the same way in Pennsylvania and Texas, you're in for a valuable surprise. The same thing applies to the way muleys are hunted in, say, Montana and Oregon. I like knowing that I can recommend this book no matter where a reader lives or hunts.

When you consult Appendix 1—a synopsis of deer distribution on this continent—you'll appreciate the other thing I'm so pleased about: the numbers of deer in America today. As noted there, the already high populations of deer are increasing in some areas, and their range is actually expanding in regions where industrialization or a spreading of the dense human population hasn't usurped the habitat.

With regard to whitetails, especially, the outlook for the near future is gratifying. The annual harvests are increasing without depleting the herds—increasing without taking more than the surplus animals that would overburden the habitat. Largely as a result of improved game management, both the harvests and the remaining deer populations have been gaining steadily in Texas, the Midwest, the Deep South, the middle Atlantic states, New England, and lower Saskatchewan and Manitoba. In "Coues Country"—New Mexico and Arizona—there has been no comparable increase but good management has stabilized the herds, as it has in eastern Canada.

The success ratios for hunters in the Great Lakes states are due to decline a little, partly because of the growing number of hunters—after all, not everyone is going to collect his deer, even if he hunts every day of the season—but also because of habitat loss. That reference to habitat loss is the first hint of the reason for the mixed emotions I mentioned.

Not long ago, John Madson collected population and harvest figures from all parts of the country and came up with some best hunting bets that bear repeating in case you're wondering whether to hunt near home next season or spend the money for a nonresident license and a trip. Highscoring whitetail states are Virginia, the Carolinas, Alabama, Georgia, Florida, Missouri, Texas, the Dakotas, and Montana.

For mule deer, the top contenders seem to be Montana, Wyoming, and

Colorado. I must add, however, that the Colorado population has evidently declined a little, as have the herds in scattered states like Oregon and Arizona. (I'm speaking of Oregon's interior mule deer, not the blacktail subspecies.) Somewhat surprisingly—in view of the highway construction and urban sprawl in much of the Midwest—the outlook in the Plains States is more encouraging. As Bert Popowski notes in Chapter 16 on the muleys of the Grain Belt, the principal land uses in large portions of those states ensure the retention of good habitat. Most authorities predict that muleys will remain stable or perhaps increase slightly in the Plains States during the next few years. It seems doubtful that they'll also increase farther south, in Texas, but they're plentiful there and likely to remain so.

The Rocky Mountain states have started tightening restrictions on non-residents (and on residents in some cases). Still more stringent restrictions are expected but I, for one, don't interpret this as an indication that the muley herds will continue to decrease in that region. They already have decreased in parts of the Rockies, and tighter hunting controls will help to keep the current numbers stable. There may, in fact, even be a slight rise if current studies lead to significant management improvements.

The Sitka blacktails seem to be abundant and stable. The Columbian blacktails are actually too abundant for the carrying capacity of the habitat in some areas. They're in excellent supply from British Columbia's coastal mountains down into California. In that state and in Oregon and Washington, the blacktails will either be stabilized or become even more plentiful in the next few years. It may actually be necessary to thin the herds (by permitting or encouraging the taking of more deer) in some locales.

The shrinkage of habitat has led in many areas to a change in the arrangements a sportsman has to make to hunt deer, and this change is likely to become ever more pronounced. I'm speaking of the trend toward the leasing of hunting rights, usually by a club, on private lands and the hunt-for-a-fee industry on additional private lands. Offhand, without rereading anything in this book, I recall both Tom Brakefield and Byron Dalrymple mentioning these trends, and similar observations by one or two other contributors may have slipped my mind. But these changes aren't the bad news I spoke of; they're merely a result of one aspect of that bad news. And in themselves they may actually be a good thing. We have to face the fact that in many regions the demands on and for land will increase. There will be sharper and sharper competition to gain control of a bit here, a bit there for everything from mining operations to housing developments for the disadvantaged. Traditionally, land that is not making money for someone (even if it is making money for the state and for conservation agencies by attracting hunters) is considered to be of little value and is easily grabbed up for all sorts of uses. But land that is making money by way of leased rights or fee hunting is likely to be maintained for that purpose, and relatively well maintained.

Better to have somewhere to hunt than nowhere.

A trend of a different but indirectly related kind is the decrease in the regularity with which big trophies are taken—especially the big mule-deer trophies. In part, this stems from the lack of time an urban sportsman has for learning how to hunt trophies. (I think it's obvious from several chapters in this book that hunting trophies isn't at all the same as just trying to take any legal deer, and a whole other book could be written on the subject of taking big trophies of several kinds.) Not only does the urban sportsman lack time and opportunity to learn real trophy-hunting; in many cases the lack of time leads to the lack of desire. But of course that's only part of the reason for the taking of fewer trophies. More important is the fact that a buck doesn't mature into a trophy in poor or limited habitat, or in a season or two. He needs time and the right kind of space. The slight gradual decline in the general muley populations has brought a sharper decline in trophies. Very obviously, some great ones are still out there, but finding them requires more effort and more know-how.

This is why I agree with the authorities who advocate the use of a guide by nonresidents in many (I'm tempted to say most) regions.

One more point: While habitat in some areas has declined, the number of hunters hasn't. Another reason fewer trophies are taken these days is that more bucks are being cropped before they reach trophy dimensions. In habitat that is overpopulated with deer, more liberal regulations to encourage the taking of does would help to alleviate this.

Part of the bad news is the interference of know-nothings in the affairs of the professional game managers. There are states in which the politically motivated legislature dictatorially controls the game department and is actually more willing to see a decline in wildlife than to chance the "bad press" that might result from the taking of more of those soft-eyed Bambi-does. In such states, more realistic regulations aren't likely in the near future. I sometimes have to wonder whether policies are determined by the elected legislators (much less the game departments) or by a few skillful antihunting propagandists working in the popular press media.

I find that in writing about trends I've run ahead of myself and already divulged another part of the bad news—continually shrinking habitat. But that, after all, is old news. The worst news is probably the complacency of hunters and hunting writers in the face of these developments. We seem to think congratulations are in order because there are more deer now than when the nation was settled and because the whitetail, especially, is a marvelously adaptable creature that can often get along with civilization. Frankly, I'm tired of reading that, and the last part of the statement is, at best, half true. In the first place, mule deer have turned out to be far less adaptable and therefore more easily hurt by the civilized sprawl that changes their habitat and even impedes seasonal migration. Whitetails don't migrate but in the northern part of the country they do need the right kind of habitat in which to yard up during the worst of the winter. And often they don't have that. In the second place, they're only so all-fired adaptable *to certain kinds of civilized encroachment.*

Many of us have complacently forgotten that the super-abundant whitetail was very close to extinction at the turn of this century. Much earlier than that, their numbers had risen sharply because timber-cutting and the clearing of farmland had replaced mature forests (which can support few deer) with the browse and cover offered by brushy second growth. But there followed the floods and slash fires and forest fires and abandonment of raped lumber tracts and, finally, the slow change from second growth back to relatively sterile forests where exploitation had left the land "worthless." There was also a slaughter of whitetails for food, hides, profit, and the protection of orchards and crops. So few whitetails were left in states like Vermont and New Jersey—which now have a great many—that whitetails were actually imported from distant regions.

Improved management and reforms in laws and law enforcement helped to restore the herds, but I wonder how many deer we would have if economic factors had not brought changes in the use of land. Today's economic factors seem less promising to the future of wildlife. And Vermont and New Jersey and a whole lot of other states still aren't remarkably progressive in their policies regarding the enhancement of habitat, the taking of does, or much else I can think of.

The very fact that deer were once endangered in this country is an indication that, with the pressures of economic growth and population growth, it could happen again. There is no reason to be complacent. The deer-hunting prospects for the foreseeable future are excellent in most regions—but only if habitat is maintained and management programs maintained or accelerated. This is a time not for complacency but for all-out support (financial, elective, and in the form of contributed time and labor—all kinds of support) of your conservation agencies and non-profit conservation societies.

If the support is sufficiently increased, the information in this book will help you to be a more successful deer hunter for many years to come.

Robert Elman
Paupack, Pennsylvania

About the Authors

As editor of this book I have the enjoyable assignment of introducing the authors (most of whom, if I may borrow an old standby of all toast-masters, need no introduction). I'm not going to give any of them star billing. They're all stars in this business of imparting hunting know-how. If one of the writers or another happens to be a favorite of yours, don't worry about his being slighted. Several of them are bigger than I am—younger, too—and I wouldn't dream of being anything but impar-tial. I'll present them in alphabetical order. I've been asked to include everyone, even myself, so I'm thankful the name Elman doesn't begin with an A. Bashline, Bauer, Brakefield, Carmichel, and Dalrymple are all bigger than I am, and besides, I'd be happy to follow them anywhere in the hunting field—not just in these pages.

Of course, being impartial doesn't mean I have to be very formal about it, or devote exactly the same space to the description of each one. I've hunted with several of these men, so I may have a little extra to say about them. The fact is I'd like to hunt with all of them. What a group they'd make if they could all get together for a whitetail or muley hunt. As a matter of fact, you might try to imagine that you're in my deer camp; some other guests are due to arrive, and you've asked me to tell you about them. It's a pleasure.

L. JAMES BASHLINE is an outdoor columnist for the Philadelphia *Inquirer,* a travel columnist for *Fly Fisherman* magazine, and a regional editor of *Field & Stream.* Readers of outdoor literature know him as an expert angler and all-round hunter, a good man to listen to whether the subject is deer or trout or wild turkeys. I hunted with Jim last season, not for deer as it happened, but for a mixed bag of upland birds. It turned out to be a bad day for pheasant, grouse, and woodcock, but he wiped my eye on ringnecks. To make matters worse, I began the day by scratching down a high, fast dove of which I was very proud until he ended the day by scoring a double on doves. Next year or the year after, I'll either get even or let bygones be bygones.

ERWIN A. BAUER (who has never revealed to me why I and most of his other friends call him "Joe") is a staff editor of *Outdoor Life,* a world-renowned nature photographer, an avid hunter and naturalist, and a hell of a nice guy. I can't remember how long I've known him, and I certainly haven't kept count of his hunting and fishing articles in all the major outdoor magazines, but I do happen to know that he's written eight books on hunting, fishing, and photography. A look at some of his close-up photos of mule deer and whitetails—taken without a telephoto lens because he wanted particularly sharp detail—tells a lot about what woods lore and stalking ability can accomplish.

TOM BRAKEFIELD is among those who are, as I mentioned, both bigger and younger than I am. He's the sort who never has to breathe hard when he strides up and down mountains carrying a hundredweight of sophisticated photographic gear. He's living up here among us damn-yankees now, but his advice about·Deep South deer hunting is based on plenty of experience; he grew up down there. He's hunted just about every kind of game and done it from Florida to Alaska. Tom is the author of the *Sportsman's Complete Book of Trophy and Meat Care* and *Big Game Hunter's Digest.* He's at work now on two more books—one about outdoor photography and one about taking trophies. His pictures and articles appear regularly in the national magazines.

JIM CARMICHEL is another transplanted Dixielander and (if you'll pardon my slight twisting of a song lyric) I've long been a number-one fan of the Man from Tennessee. When he isn't off on safari somewhere, he lives in Arizona these days. He's shooting editor of *Outdoor Life,* a noted big-game hunter, and a winner of high honors in competitive target shooting with both rifle and shotgun. I like to talk about Jim's fame because I not only knew him when, but was one of the first editors to recognize his abilities. That was long ago, when he was working with the Tennessee Game and Fish Commission. He once told me that if I hadn't bought one of his early stories he might have quit and become some kind of wealthy business tycoon, but I'm damned if I'll say I'm sorry. Jim is author of an excellent Winchester Press book, *The Modern Rifle.*

BYRON W. DALRYMPLE is a hunter, fisherman, camper, photographer, and writer whose pictures and articles have been welcomed by millions of readers of outdoor magazines for about three decades. He must have gone the distance from short pants to success in about one quick hop, because I can remember reading his stories and admiring his photos when I was a kid probing the mysteries of squirrel hunting, and he doesn't look that much older than I am. When it comes to deer, Byron ought to be awarded a Doctorate of Hunting Knowledge. He was the first man ever to write in any detail about the Carmen Mountains whitetail of the Big Bend Country. (As a matter of fact, he may be the only man to have written detailed articles about them.) He's extremely adept at rattling up Texas whitetail bucks—a technique he describes in Chapter 12 on Southwestern hunting—and he's no slouch at putting the scope on muleys, either.   He's also the author of the deservedly popular book *North American Big Game Hunting*.

ROBERT ELMAN is—well, let's see, there must be something to say about him besides the obvious notation that he's the editor of this book.   I'm not too comfortable writing about myself in the third person, so I'll switch from "he" to "I."   I've written close to a dozen books and edited others, most of them about hunting, fishing, firearms, nature study, or some other aspect of outdoor living.   I've also written a lot of magazine articles and edited magazines dealing with the same topics. Over the years I have stepped in beaver holes and gone sprawling in near-freezing water, forgotten my knife, and fallen asleep on stand, yet somehow harvested a bit of venison, so I qualify as a deer-hunting editor and writer.   I also happen to know all these other deer-hunting writers and was therefore able to get them all together in this book.   It's no bad thing to bask in their reflected glory.

DR. SAM FADALA reminds me of the way the great Teddy Roosevelt became an outdoorsman.   Like Roosevelt, Sam was a more or less urban Easterner with a boyhood malady that required an outdoor cure.   He was born in Albany, New York, and moved out to Tucson, where the desert sun and clear, dry air remedied his chronic asthma. Inevitably he became intrigued by hunting.   Although he's put in long and successful stints as a teacher (he holds the M.A. degree in teaching from the University of Alaska and a doctorate in education from the University of Arizona), he's now a full-time outdoor writer.   His work has appeared in *Sports Afield, Outdoor Life, Field & Stream, The American Rifleman, The American Hunter,* and other well-known outdoor magazines.   Sam's wife Nancy loves to hunt, and they spend vacations with their three children camping or hunting.   A lucky man, Sam Fadala.

STEVE FERBER tells funnier stories than any other guest I've had at my hunting camp.   Less important, but I suppose still worth mentioning, is the fact that he's listed in the *Who's Who of Sports* and the *New York Times Record Book of Sports* because he's won over a thousand trophies in rifle, pistol, and shotgun competitions, established sixteen national shooting records, and (when he was a member and coach of the U.S. Navy Shooting Team) was awarded the Distinguished Pistol Shooter's Badge by the Secretary of the Navy.   Several years ago he was also awarded the shooting editorship of *Argosy,* but now he heads his own company, Aqua-Field Publications, which edits and publishes high-quality outdoor annuals.   Practicing what he preaches, he used a pistol to take a very nice muley this year, and I can testify that it furnished excellent venison.

B. R. HUGHES was, to the best of my knowledge, a simple free-lance writer when I first became acquainted with his work. Bill's still a free-lance writer and a busy one, but he's also associate editor of *Gun Week* and shotgun editor of both *Gunsport* and *Gun Collector*. Furthermore, he's editor of *The Muzzleloader,* a magazine to which I've had the pleasure of contributing articles on historic firearms. Like the rest of us, he's harvested both whitetails and mule deer with conventional rifles; and like not quite so many of us, he's also taken those and many other kinds of game, large and small, with muzzleloading arms. Sam Fadala isn't the only teacher in our group, as Bill has taught college courses in journalism. He's been published in most of the leading magazines dealing with guns, hunting, and target shooting.

JOHN MADSON has taken me bird-shooting at the Winchester Conservation Department's experimental farm in Nilo, Illinois, thus joining Jim Bashline and the ranks of others who have wiped my eye. I manage to bear him no malice, however, as he's a good friend, a considerate sportsman, a genuine authority on wildlife, and one of our best hunting writers. He's the Assistant Director of Conservation for Winchester-Western. He's also the author of a number of small but information-packed books on various game species, published by the Winchester Conservation Department, which have become classics of their kind. (And those who know me are aware that I don't often use that overworked word "classic.") Appendix 2 in this volume—on field-dressing and other important post-kill matters—is adapted from one of those books, straightforwardly entitled *The White-Tailed Deer.* John has written a great many articles for the outdoor press and has earned the Jade of Chiefs Award, the highest honor bestowed by the Outdoor Writers Association of America.

DON MCKNIGHT is one of the only two contributors who are not familiar to most readers of outdoor magazines. (I'll introduce the other one next.) Don isn't a professional writer, but his chapter on the Sitka blacktail certainly proves he's a natural-born writer. When I was deciding which species and subspecies to assign to which contributors, I had no trouble at all in matching the more widespread varieties of deer to appropriate authors. The career outdoor writers have done plenty of whitetail hunting and have also had impressive experience with what might be called "conventional" mule deer. But the Sitka blacktail is limited in distribution and inhabits country far from the contiguous states. A few writers had hunted Sitka blacktails once or twice while on trips to Alaska, but they said candidly that they didn't know much about this deer. So I asked Tom Brakefield, who had recently returned from Alaska, to put me in touch with a real expert on Sitka blacktails. "How about D. E.

McKnight?'' he asked. "Don is a Research Chief for the Division of Game in the Alaska Department of Fish and Game. And he's done plenty of work with blacktails. He's a good hunter, too. I don't think you can get much more expert than that.'' He was right.

DAVID NAMIAS deals in art, not words. He devised the fine range maps that appear in Appendix 1, showing the distribution of whitetails and mule deer on this continent. As an art assistant for a major publisher, he's worked with a number of outdoor writers (including me) on books about hunting, fishing, and natural history. When I decided an appendix was needed to clarify the distribution of species, I immediately thought of him, because I'd been impressed by some previous mapping he'd done to show American wildlife ranges. You may have seen his work before without knowing who did it, so I'm pleased to introduce him to you.

NORM NELSON was a Minnesota newspaper editor for more than sixteen years, but he's lived in the State of Washington for the past decade. He'd been an avid outdoorsman in the Midwest, and he continues to pursue the same activities on the Pacific Coast, where he's Resource Information Manager for the Weyerhaeuser Company. When I last spoke to Norm, he'd written 75 articles for *Field & Stream, Outdoor Life, Sports Afield, Gun Digest. The American Rifleman. The American Hunter.* and so on. He's also contributed to several anthologies. By the time this volume is published, his score will have risen and I can't predict how many Nelson stories will have been published. Plenty is my closest estimate. Norm lives in a good region for any deer hunter; without going far from home, he can hunt whitetails and blacktails as well as what I've called "conventional" mule deer—and he's hunted all three varieties successfully. For that matter, he's hunted many kinds of game in many parts of the country, which is why readers know they can trust his advice.

DAVID PETZAL is managing editor of *Field & Stream.* He's also the author of *The .22 Rifle* and editor of two fine anthologies, *The Expert's Book of the Shooting Sports* and *The Expert's Book of Upland Game and Waterfowl Hunting.* And Dave's an old friend whose wry wit has lightened my burden in publishing offices, on hunts, and over long business lunches at which the shop talk of other colleagues had me climbing the menu. When I first knew Dave, he was a fine target rifleman and chuck hunter but only a casual shotgunner. Several other friends and I somehow got him interested in shotgunning, and he soon became better with a scattergun than I'll ever be. Similarly, when I first knew him he was more enthralled with chucks than with big game, but he had the woodsmanship and the marksmanship with a rifle to make a fine big-game hunter. He has now taken more deer (and more of the bigger game species) than I have. It's a delight to be with him in the field or in print.

BERT POPOWSKI decided many years ago that he wanted to live near what he loved most—wildlife.   So he built himself a cabin surrounded by it.   There in his South Dakota woods his immediate neighbors include deer, wild turkeys, rabbits, and assorted other small game, trout, and waterfowl.   And not far away are the pronghorns that helped to make him famous.   One of his books, *Hunting Pronghorn Antelope,* added tremendously to the popularity of his writings when it was published in 1959, and since then it has gained status as the standard in the field.   He's written other books, of course, on a variety of subjects, including game calling and crow shooting.   And he has long been a contributing editor to *The American Rifleman,* in which capacity he's one of the elite group of experts who represent the National Rifle Association by answering readers' questions about firearms and hunting.   One of Bert's sons works with the state's conservation department and is thus carrying on the Popowski outdoor tradition.   Come to think of it, I've been told Bert's hunting prowess is, in itself, a South Dakota tradition.

LEONARD LEE RUE III has probably taught me more about wildlife and the outdoors in general than any other man.   It wasn't that he was trying to dust my mind for cobwebs or that I was looking for an instructor.   It was just that no one could hunt with Len—or even just walk through the woods and fields with him—and not learn something.   He's the most observant hunter I've ever been with.   I don't think a nibbled twig escapes his attention.   And his consistent hunting success proves he knows how to read signs.   Most of my hunts with him have been for pheasant, yet each outing added to my understanding of deer and other game.   He's the author of *Cottontail, The World of the White-Tailed Deer, The World of the Red Fox,* and *Pictorial Guide to the Birds of North America,* among other books.   He's also one of the nation's finest wildlife photographers; his pictures appear regularly in *Audubon* and *National Wildlife,* as well as many other magazines.

NORMAN STRUNG is a very professional outdoor writer—an outdoor writer's outdoor writer.   But he doesn't do it full-time, because he insists on devoting a large part of his energy and time to being a licensed Montana hunting and fishing guide.   Norm could just write for a living, but he'd rather put up with a few more dudes and a few less editors.   Which reminds me: I mentioned that Dave Petzal has killed more deer (I think) than I have, and if my memory is correct, at least one of his muleys was taken on a trip with Norm.   I don't know if that's of particular interest to anyone in the world except Norm Strung and Dave Petzal, but I'll include it to help out their future biographers.   Getting back to Norm's writing, one of his books is a favorite of mine—*Misty Mornings and Moonless Nights: A Waterfowler's Guide.*   Norm obviously knows how to hunt ducks and geese as well as deer. He writes for all the major outdoor magazines, and he's a director of the Outdoor Writers Association of America (to which I owe dues that I will pay, Norm, I promise, as soon as I get a check for my own next magazine story and pay off a taxidermist to whom I wouldn't owe money anyway if it weren't for a guide who reminds me of you).

RUSSELL TINSLEY is probably a little sore at me. When I was giving out assignments I called him just on the chance that he'd probably done a lot of deer hunting with a bow. He sounded a little surprised when he asked me if I hadn't read any of his accounts of same, or seen any of his photos on the subject. I had to admit that I read so much material of this nature that sometimes it blurs together. But I knew he'd done plenty of deer hunting and recalled that he'd once written a story for me about whitetails. I also knew he was an archer, so I wasn't far off base. What's more, I knew how he became an archer: Russ is an exceptionally fine varmint caller, and anyone who can bring raccoons and coyotes and foxes and such within rock-tossing distance is going to be tempted to try bowhunting. He's an outdoor columnist for the Austin, Texas, *American Statesman*. He's also the author of seven books on outdoor activities, and the editor of an eighth, a new Winchester Press book called *All About Small Game Hunting in America*. I don't know how many magazine articles he's written. I don't even know how many he wrote for me when I was a magazine editor. A lot, though.

LEONARD M. WRIGHT, JR. is a problem writer. If your only outdoor interest is hunting, you may never have read any of his work. Len insists that he's first an angler, second a hunter, and third a promotion executive for the New York *Times*. Len has written a great many articles for magazines ranging from *Esquire* to the best-known outdoor publications. He's also the author of a somewhat scholarly sounding but brilliantly helpful how-to book called *Fishing the Dry Fly as a Living Insect*, as well as a new Winchester Press book with the less-ponderous, more-to-the-point title of *Fly-Fishing Heresies*. Great. But as far as I know, he never wrote a blessed thing about anything except fishing—nothing at all about one of his consummate skills: deer hunting. After a day of hunting deer (or grouse and woodcock a little earlier in the fall) I've spent many an hour arguing with him. He felt I wasn't doing enough writing about fishing. I felt he was eccentric (though I may have used a stronger term in discussions with him as he poured me another three fingers) to ignore hunting in his writings. Obviously, I've finally won the argument.

PART I

Arms and Approaches

1

Arms and the Game

by David Petzal

Anyone who has spent some time in a deer camp is aware of the following indisputable facts: The lever-action carbine is the only fit gun for a whitetail hunter.   The lever-action carbine is inaccurate and underpowered, and any deer killed with one is a victim of extreme bad luck.   The scoped, bolt-action rifle is as out of place in deer woods as a Grand Prix racing car in city traffic.   The scoped, bolt-action rifle is the only arm powerful and accurate enough to drop deer dependably under all circumstances.   Buckshot is worthless.   Buckshot is deadly . . . and on, and on.

The reason for these contradictory opinions, I think, is that deer hunters are like the blind men describing the elephant.   Each man is convinced that the part he touched is what an elephant is really like.   Similarly, there are different ways to hunt deer, and the guns and cartridges that work best for each technique differ considerably.   That's why, as you read this book, you'll find that some of the other authors disagree with certain of my opinions.   In some cases they may disagree with one another, too.   But bear in mind that they're all experts.   What you're getting here isn't the view of a single hunter but the views of many authorities.   You'll just have to think hard about the opinions (as well as the out and out facts, which won't prompt much disagreement) and decide which of them will be most relevant to your kind of deer hunting.   But before we get into the technical end of things, let's take a look at this creature we're hunting.   Or rather, two creatures.   First we'll discuss the whitetail, then the mule deer.

Contrary to what most tyros believe, the whitetail is neither large nor tough nor tenacious of life.   A respectable buck will weigh 150 pounds on the hoof, and I'd guess that the average mature male goes 20 pounds less.   Does are even smaller.   Whitetails' hides are not thick, and they lack the massive layers of muscle that make their larger relatives, elk, so hard to drop.   So the first conclusion we can draw about whitetail arms and cartridges is that, obviously, you don't need a really powerful rifle or a tough-jacketed bullet that offers great penetration..

Indeed, I think the single greatest cause of lost deer—poor marksmanship aside—is the use by hunters of heavy bullets designed for larger game. There is, for example, a great difference between the 180- and 150-grain bullet in cartridges such as the .30/06 and .308. The heavier projectile opens up far more slowly, and is suited for game such as elk and moose. On encountering a whitetail, these bullets expand hardly at all, punch their way completely through, and expend very little of their force inside the animal, where it should be spent. A whitetail with a pencil-size hole through its lungs will die eventually, but it will run a long way before it does, and it will not leave much of a blood trail.

A thinner-jacketed 150-grain bullet, traveling at higher speed, will penetrate the hide and then expand, violently. It will probably not exit, but then it won't have to, because a deer struck in the lungs or the heart with such a bomb will do only one thing—drop.

This is one valid argument against the so-called "deer" cartridges such as the .30/30, .32 Special, and .35 Remington. The first of these (the second is even less effective) pushes a 150-grain bullet at 2,400 fps. The .30/06, in comparison, drives a bullet of the same weight a full 500 fps faster. The slower velocity is just not sufficient to impart quick expansion to a bullet of any type, and things are made worse by the fact that many ill-informed hunters use 170-grain .30/30 loads, which move out at only 2,200 fps. The .35 Remington is a little better. Its ballistics are the same, but by virtue of its larger bullet diameter, it punches a slightly bigger hole.

So why, you ask, have so many million lever-action carbines been sold, and why do so many people still use them? The answer is twofold: First, the .30/30 was considered a red-hot high-velocity cartridge . . . 60 years ago. Second, and more important, the light, short-barreled, fast-shooting guns chambered for it are wonderfully handy in the dense, brushy country that whitetails inhabit. A lot of these guns were sold because they were the best there was at the time. They're still wonderfully handy, but are they still the best or is much of their attraction a matter of tradition? These guns come equipped with open iron sights that are next to worthless and, on many of them, scope mounting is a problem. Rear peep sights on these guns would be fine, except that many of the people who buy them are not sophisticated enough to have such sights installed. With fine modern rifles available from the very same manufacturers, you can see why the old thutty-thutty does not get a warm recommendation from this source.

Short, light, quick-handling guns are indispensible to one of the two tactics that deer hunters use—still-hunting. Still-hunters are in nearly

Waiting on stand in this kind of whitetail country, you may get a shot at a deer a dozen yards away or more than 100 yards off. You want a rifle that can perform properly in either situation—not the sort of heavy-barreled varminter with a high-powered scope that's sometimes used for open-country muley hunting, and not something that fires a big, heavy, relatively slow bullet touted to be a "brush-buster" but ballistically second-rate.

constant motion, and because of this, when a deer is spotted, things happen fast. You may kick one out of a tangled thicket and have no more time to draw a bead on it than has a grouse hunter to swing on a partridge. So the last thing you want is a 10-pound rifle with a 24-inch barrel and a 6× scope. Speed is of the essence.

I tend to favor autoloaders over levers or pumps because their gas-operated actions soften recoil, and that, together with the fact that you don't have to pump or lever anything, allows you to get off a quicker second shot.

There are a number of excellent autoloaders on the market—Browning, H&R, Remington, Ruger, and Winchester all make good ones—chambered for a wide variety of appropriate cartridges, including .270, .280, .308, .30/06 and .44 Magnum. All of these will do just fine.

But what of that second piece of ordnance we mentioned at the outset, the scoped, bolt-action rifle? Well, it's what I use, and what most of the people I hunt with use. This type of arm places a premium on *precision*, on driving one shot right where you want it, at short and long range alike.

The other style of deer hunting—sit and wait—is the province of the precision shooter. When you're moving, the odds are against your seeing a whitetail before he sees you (unless there's soft snow on the ground, or the woods are wet, or you're a skillful stalker, or any combination of these). Very often, it makes sense to lurk, especially if the woods are full of hunters who are keeping the deer moving.

So find a comfortable stump to lean against, making sure there's some brush near you to break up your outline, and that you have a clear field of fire. Your stand may overlook a deer trail, and your shot may be taken at only 25 yards, or it may open on an apple orchard 100 yards distant or a power line right-of-way where venison may appear 300 yards off.

If this is your approach to the sport, what you want is an accurate bolt-action in any caliber from .243 or 6mm up through .30/06. Nothing smaller, nothing bigger. Them what uses 7mm and .30 Magnums on whitetails are kidding themselves. I have killed my share of deer with Magnum rifles, and I can testify that they drop no faster from a .300 Weatherby than from a .30/06. More important, the .300 has a 24-inch barrel, should weigh about nine pounds if it's not to tear your shoulder off, kicks more, and has far more muzzle blast than the smaller gun. For bigger game the Magnums are great, but not for whitetail.

As long as you stick to the standard calibers, I believe the choice of cartridge is not so important as the choice of bullet. For example, if you're using a 6mm, don't use the 80-grain projectile, which is strictly for varmints and will blow up on a deer's hide. Take the trouble to read the information on the ammunition box before you buy it, and make note of the type of game for which it's intended. If you're a handloader, all of the major bullet companies supply excellent data on the construction and design of their various slugs.

A word or two about sights: Scopes are better than iron sights in just about all circumstances, and low-powered scopes are better than high-powered ones which, for whitetail hunting, are useless. A scope offers the following advantages over iron sights (both open and peep): It puts both the sighting device—the reticle—and the target on the same optical plane, which enables you to keep everything in focus. At dawn and twilight, it actually gathers light. And, perhaps most important, the magnification allows you to see just what you're shooting at: buck or doe, deer or cow, good head or mediocre.

I have been able, using a 4× scope, to look *into* dense brush and pick out the outline of a deer, simply because the magnified image enabled me to discern an ear or an antler. You can't do that with iron sights. And of course, for a long shot, a scope is invaluable.

Of all magnifications, the 4× is by far the most popular for general big-game hunting, but for the whitetail I don't think it's the best you can do. My vote goes to the 1×–4× or 1.5×–5× variable which, from my experience, is vastly superior to everything else. When it's cranked down to its lowest power, you can see the whole world and pick up on a running buck with no hesitation. When it's turned up to a higher degree of magnification, you enjoy all the benefits of a fixed-power scope.

The one drawback to these instruments, aside from an extra ounce or two of weight, is the fact that they cost a good deal more than fixed powers. So if budget limitations are a problem, I'd suggest you look at a 2½×, 2¾×, or 3× model.

As for reticles, again the choice is simple. I, and it seems most others, prefer the Duplex reticle originated by Leupold and offered by other scope manufacturers under a variety of names. This reticle consists of very heavy crosshairs which taper abruptly at the center of the lens. They draw the eye to the intersection of the wires, and this enables you to pick up a target quickly, and/or in poor light. The fine wires at the center allow you to shoot at distant targets without the crosshairs subtending too much.

I should add that every whitetail hunter would do well to add to his gear a set of compact binoculars of either 6× or 7× magnification. There are probably a dozen glasses on the market that are optically excellent, weigh but a few ounces, and fit in a shirt pocket. Unless you are strictly of the walk-and-kick-'em-up school, good binoculars will prove invaluable. They are far, far better for identifying distant objects than a rifle scope. And consider this: If the critter you think may be a deer turns out to be a man, would you rather make the discovery through a scope or with binoculars?

In some areas, rifles are forbidden for deer hunting, and you are constrained to use either rifled slugs or buckshot. If the area in question specifies buckshot only, you might think about hunting somewhere else unless you restrict your shots to 25 yards or so. Sorry about that, but my own experiments and those of people whose objectivity I respect have shown that beyond that 00 buck does not pattern consistently enough to ensure clean kills.

Happily, rifled slugs are a different matter. In a slug barrel with good sights, they are extremely accurate up to 75 yards, and occasionally you'll get an exceptional gun that will shoot them accurately at 100 yards. If you are serious about collecting a deer with rifled slugs, as opposed to just taking an optimistic walk in the woods with a shotgun, I suggest that you get a pump or autoloader with a slug barrel. The nice thing about this arrangement is that such a gun can be equipped with a variety of other barrels as well, and can earn its keep at a number of different pursuits.

I have done considerable shooting with a 12-gauge pump gun equipped with a slug barrel and a 2× intermediate-eye-relief scope, and found it to be far more accurate, within its range limitations, than any whitetail would ever require. Slug barrels come equipped with open sights, which are a hell of a lot better than a plain shotgun bead, but if you can arrange to have a low-power scope mounted on your scattergun you are way ahead of the game. Some states allow you to hunt deer with a 20-gauge slug. Don't. It is at best a marginal projectile, and the 12 is far better.

Mule deer are a different story. Whereas the average shot at a whitetail is probably taken at something less than 100 yards, I'd estimate that the typical mule-deer trophy is collected at 200. Whitetails are creatures of the dense woods and thickets; muleys are residents of the forests

LEFT: The author refuses to call this an ideal whitetail rifle, but he says it comes very close—which may surprise some readers because it's a .30/06. It's a custom job, stocked in the Mannlicher style, with a Springfield action and a 20-inch barrel, and mounted with a 2¾× scope. (The .30/06 has been found to be deadly on mule deer, too; it comes close to being the mythical ''all-around'' sporter.)

RIGHT: This .280 is another custom-built rifle. The scope is a 2×–7× variable. Petzal gives this sort of combination high marks as a mule-deer rifle.

and sage flats of the West. You may get a close shot at a muley, but the odds are more likely that you'll get a long one.

These big-eared critters are larger than whitetails. A good mature buck will run upwards of 150 pounds, and 200-plus-pounders are not at all rare. But like whitetails, they are not made of steel, so the same remarks apply . . . almost. Muleys are a little tougher because of their greater size, but not much.

For this reason, I would not take a .243 or a 6mm mule-deer hunting. I have seen a number of these animals shot quite dead with these cartridges, but the kills were made at close range. Out at long yardages, these two numbers lack the steam I like.

I hesitate to say that anything is "ideal" for any type of game, but where mule deer are concerned, you just can't do any better than a .270. This cartridge has it all: flat trajectory, mild recoil, and great killing power. Way out on the prairie, as the song goes, if you were to check all

Here are three cartridges Dave Petzal considers tops for both whitetails and mule deer. They are, from left, the .270, .280, and .30/06. He cautions against overweight bullets in the cartridge of your choice, and the text offers specific recommendations.

the rifles riding around in pickup trucks, I'd guess that the .270 would come in far ahead of everything else in popularity.

However, I would be remiss if I did not point out that there are a few other cartridges which may be as good, if not as popular. These are the .25/06 with the 120-grain bullet, the .280 with the 150-grainer, .284 with the same weight projectile, and the .30/06 with the 150- or the new 165-grain bullet. The chances are that you could shoot mule deer the rest of your life with these and never notice any real difference in effectiveness. It's just that the .270 has been around longer, and ammo in this caliber can be bought in every gas station and hardware store west of the Mississippi. For mule deer only, I prefer it with the 130-grain bullet, but for hunting where there are elk, I'd select the 150-grain load.

Glassing for distant mule deer is a common hunting method in many parts of the country, whether you're in the mountains or on the plains or deserts. Obviously, where this technique is productive you need a good binocular, a good scope, and an accurate, flat-shooting rifle.

Guide and noted outdoor writer Norm Strung grins happily over a muley buck felled by a single lung shot from a .270 at about 200 yards. After being hit, the deer trotted perhaps 100 yards and keeled over. Clean one-shot kills of this sort are what rifle choice is all about.

Since much of your shooting will be at long range, you'll want the most accurate rifle possible, and speed of fire will take a back seat. Here the bolt-action has no real competition. I would suggest only that before you use the rifle seriously, you have a gunsmith tune up the trigger. For some reason, most bolt-actions have excellent adjustable trigger mechanisms which are not excellently adjusted at the factory. Why this is I dunno, but most of them need adjustment as they come out of the factory box. A good bolt-action trigger should break at three to four pounds, and break clean, with no creep or drag.

As for sights, nobody uses iron anymore, and just about everyone seems to use the 4× scope. I really can't disagree with this choice, except to volunteer the information that I've found a 2×–7× variable to be highly useful. But all things considered, the 4× is just about tops.

On occasion, I have seen misguided souls lugging rifles equipped with 3×–9× variables, which are bulky and heavy. The last thing you want out West, where mountains are mountains and distances are on the long side, is a heavy rifle on your shoulder. (And while we're on the subject, you would have to chase me for a long time to give me a mule-deer rifle that weighed more than 8¼ pounds, scoped, loaded, with sling—the main reason I rule out the Magnums. Rifles for them are just too damn heavy.)

Reticle choice? The Duplex, or one like it. Just remember that all the firearms expertise in the world won't help you collect a muley if you can't hike and can't shoot accurately.

Need I add that you should practice with the rifle of your choice? Strange to say, many, many hunters sight-in their guns from a benchrest and sally forth, convinced that they are the spiritual descendants of Davy Crockett. Naturally, when they have to shoot offhand or sitting, they are slow, shaky, and miss. So, shades of the late Mr. Crockett, or Boone, or Carson, or whoever you prefer, get out to the range each year well ahead of the season, and expend a few boxes of cartridges. Shoot from your hind legs, and concentrate on getting on target quickly and shooting quickly. The deer isn't going to give you more than a split second, and that's all you should need. Remember, good game shots shoot quickly.

2

The Art of
Still-Hunting

by Leonard M. Wright, Jr.

Frankly, I've never thought the term "still-hunting" was a very good choice to describe the type of deer hunting I know and like best. It sounds far too stationary to me. "Slow-hunting" or "quiet-hunting" might have been far better, but it's probably too late to quibble over definitions.

What we refer to as "still-hunting" is really stop-and-go hunting. A step, a long careful look, then another step. At its fastest pace, which is permissible in wet woods or when crossing an unproductive opening, it may approach a slow mosey. It is only partly still, but it is all hunting.

Still-hunting is, I'm proud to say, as American as apple pie, installment buying, and the roadside disposable beer can. Unlike most other kinds of hunting, it has no European heritage; it evolved in our Northeast two or three hundred years ago simply because it was the best way to hunt whitetail deer in that terrain.

If the rich or the nobility had settled America, an early American deer hunt would have been more like a Virginia fox hunt. Only those to the manor born were allowed to hunt deer in England or on the Continent in those days, and the exercise was a very social horses-and-hounds affair. Most early American settlers were less pretentious people who tried to claw a living out of the rocky soil and, to them, venison was a diet staple rather than the by-product of a gala event.

Certainly, these early farmers ambushed deer at dusk near their orchards or gardens, tracked and ran them down, torchlighted them after dark, trapped them, took them any way they could. But after the crops had been harvested, the few easy deer had been skimmed off and it was time to hang the winter's supply of meat, these early hunters had to leave the farm in the valley floor and pursue the deer up through their hillside woodlots and on into the mountains above. This was a part-time effort, not a business (the winter wood had to be sawed and split, too), so the

32

This is the toughest kind of still-hunting—walking through dry woods. To keep noise down, it may be necessary to skirt brushy thickets—merely looking into them carefully from more open parts of the woods—but if you go along slowly and quietly enough, and do enough stopping and looking, and pay attention to the direction of the breeze and the probable location of deer at a given time of day, you may well jump a buck at close range.

hunter, usually alone, had to get the most venison per hour or it could be a lean winter indeed.

This type of hunter couldn't travel far and, in fact, he didn't need to. There were enough deer within a half-mile—or at most a mile—of his farm to feed his family. But without a retinue of serfs, hounds, and horses, how could he best harvest this crop? Playing the deer's own game, on the deer's terms and in the deer's own backyard—which is what still-hunting is all about—turned out to be the answer.

Admittedly, this is not a trophy-hunting technique, although it has certainly accounted for its share of the deer heads you see on walls. It is mainly a practical way to take an average buck with an occasional rack thrown in as a surprise bonus for the patient hunter. However, skill is rewarded and error punished to a very high degree in this type of hunting. A novice may blunder onto a big buck at dawn on opening day, but over the years, a skilled practitioner will outproduce him ten to one.

I'd love to take you along on some memorable still-hunts in words and pictures right now, but that would be more an indulgence to me than a help to you. I have too many hard-core, how-to details to cover before we can relax and reminisce by the fireplace after a successful hunt.

First, there is the matter of equipment. Fortunately, the gear needed for this type of deer hunting is pleasantly undemanding and most farmers or country-dwellers probably have most items or reasonable facsimiles already at hand. Look through your own inventory of outdoor clothes and see how much of the following you can lay your hands on.

Starting at the bottom and working up brings us first to the all-important matter of footwear. I hold that boots should be at least 12 inches high and utterly waterproof. Some say their leather boots keep their feet absolutely dry, but I've never been lucky enough to own such a pair. The same goes for pacs. I no longer take chances. I struggle along in a pair of lace-up rubber boots that reach just above my calves. Not the most comfortable footwear, but I'm not going to cover much mileage and the added insurance against any leakage plays a vital part in some of my hunts, as we shall see.

A heavy pair of socks (or two light pairs) are all that's necessary for warmth. You'll be moving around just enough to avoid cold feet and will have no need to bundle up your toes excessively as long as your socks are made of wool. Synthetic or cotton socks may look thick and comfy, but they don't do much for you when they get damp and feet are sure to sweat some inside rubber boots. So much so, in fact, that I usually carry a spare pair of wools for a comfort change halfway through the day.

I like wool pants, too. Medium-weight will do if worn over a pair of long johns. You might need those heavy, feltlike blanket-pants if you're going on stand for an hour or more in late November, but I've rarely felt the need for them while still-hunting.

My midriff and upper body seem happier in wool, too. A light wool sweater, with or without sleeves, makes a fine undershirt. Over this I wear a light wool shirt topped off with a heavy red wool shirt, and this is sufficient for most days. When the mercury starts out below zero and looks as if it will stay there all day, I substitute a down jacket with a red overvest for the heavy wool shirt.

Warm hands are crucial and on the bitterest days I wear fleece-lined mittens. I can slip off the right one quickly enough when I need to shoot. My hat is red, orange, or yellow, has a visor against the sun, and fold-down earflaps. And that about covers it—or me.

I do carry a few accessories, though—extra cartridges, yellow shooting glasses, a light pocketknife with a sharp three-inch blade in case this is my lucky day, a six-foot piece of light nylon rope for the same reason, and some sort of sandwich or quick-energy candy bar. If more trinkets mean more fun to you, by all means carry them. A small compass and topo maps will be welcome if you're in strange territory (which you shouldn't be if you're still-hunting the best way possible).

And, oh yes, you'll need a gun, too, won't you? Any rifle-and-sight combination that will allow you to kill a deer surely and quickly at, say, 125 yards is perfectly adequate.

Naturally, I have a personal preference and good reasons to back it up. I carry a .30/06. Overkill, many say, but I rarely have to use a second shot. This one is a very light sporterized Mauser that weighs little more than a good .22. On top of this is mounted a 3× scope with a post reticle. This is plenty of magnification for up to 150 yards and the post is easier to pick up in the dark woods than fine crosshairs. For insurance, I have an open peep sight set just below this in case snow, fog, or rain fouls up my scope or in case I have to take a shot at a jumped deer.

This latter contingency I have avoided all but once or twice in my life. I am against chance shots at running deer in thick woods. A wild shot can clear the nearby woods for an hour or two. But, even worse, a gut- or rump-shot deer may die a mile or two (and three posted boundaries) away and this is surely a mug's game. Admittedly, I do have a friend who can kill a running deer nine times out of ten. He has four Purple Hearts, slept with his rifle for four years, and by the way he shoots I'm not sure he still doesn't take the thing to bed with him. Frankly, I can't shoot that well myself.

Anyway, now that you're fully equipped, where do you hunt? Any hilly or rolling country with semi-open woods will do. Hardwoods, or mainly hardwood forests, are best. If you can't see 50 yards you're probably better off driving deer to standers or jump-shooting deer with buckshot (where legal) or rifled slugs. On the other hand, if you can see more than 150 yards the woods are probably too thin for good still-hunting. Most hardwood stands fall between these two densities and this is where the still-hunter reigns supreme. Look at the best deer country in your area and, unless you live in the Southwest or in open, grassy cattle country, you'll be surprised how much prime hunting territory falls into this category.

If the chosen section of woods is overrun with hunters, you may do better standing (and probably shivering) at a likely place and letting the others push the deer to you. But if you're the only hunter on a 100- to 400-acre tract, you'll usually see a lot more deer by actively searching them out.

Even if you're alone, don't confuse this with the wilderness hunting you've read about in books. The deer will be smart and wise to the ways of man and will have set up feeding and traveling patterns to cash in on man's crops with a minimum of contact. If you know the feeding areas,

An ultimate challenge of still-hunting is to become such an adept stalker that you can do what the photographer did to get this picture—walk right up on a bedded buck. (Photo: Illinois, Dept. of Conservation)

the bedding areas, the best-used trails, you're way ahead of the game.   And if you know the woods like the back of your hand, you won't waste time glassing stumps or blowdowns.   For these reasons, you'll be many times more effective still-hunting an area you know really well.   If you're invited to shoot new territory, try to walk it and know it before the season starts if at all possible.   Familiarity breeds venison.

Early and late in the day are prime times—early has the edge—but since still-hunting is a percentage game, it's worth your while to hunt as much of the day as possible. It pays to be well into the woods and away from houses or roads by the time legal shooting starts. Here's where the yellow shooting glasses pay off. They help you see in very dim light and they protect your eyes from twigs you'll never see at that time of day. They'll do the same on your way out at dusk, too.

Once into prime hunting territory, it's usually best to hunt on a level course, or cross-hill, for the first hour or two. Deer drift up from the valley floor where they have been night-feeding until daybreak. One of your best chances of the day is intercepting them from above. As the morning wears on, however, it may pay to work diagonally higher up the slopes to catch up with deer that may have slipped by you earlier in the day. Reverse the process as dusk approaches.

Those are only general rules. Weather should influence your tactics as much as time of day. When it's stormy, deer may stay just above the valley floor all day and not go back up to their usual bedding areas. And in very cold weather—the best, but least comfortable, still-hunting weather—deer will have to move around and feed all day to stay warm. Again, knowing your acreage and the habits of the deer that inhabit it are priceless advantages.

Now that you've arrived at the right place at the right time, you can finally get down to the hunting itself. The two most important questions here are: How fast (or slowly) should you move? And how can you see deer before they see you?

There are no pat answers because your tactics should change with conditions. But there are some basics that apply to all conditions. First, move much more slowly than you think you have to. And second, try to move upwind or, if you have to zigzag back and forth, try to approach the choicest spots upwind. The chief reason for this approach is that deer can't hear you nearly as well when the wind blows from them to you. I'll now stick my neck way out and say that I don't believe your scent is the governing factor here. I'm convinced that for every deer that hightails it because he has picked up your odor, there are ten that have departed because they've picked up the noise created by your big flat feet.

When the woods are wet, you can move at a fair, steady pace. Dead leaves are quiet and since the forest floor is bare of snow you can even avoid stepping on twigs. But don't let twig-dodging keep you from looking ahead and around. And be sure to look farther ahead than you usually do. In fact, this is a basic rule for still-hunting under all conditions.

We all tend to look at, or focus on, the trees, landmarks, or clearings that are easily visible. This habit must be broken, because it just won't do for still-hunting. Strain to examine the outer limits that you can't really see properly.   That's where the deer will be and every few steps will open up a whole new world of these outer limits.   Any place you can see clearly and easily has been vacated by deer minutes before.   Count on it.

Fresh snow underfoot is the next easiest condition.   Dead leaves won't make any noise and deer will stand out better against the white background, but go slowly.   You can't see twigs on small branches and when you step on them, they'll sound like rifle shots to both you and the deer.   There's a great temptation to follow a seemingly fresh set of tracks under these conditions, but I've found it rarely pays off. Half-hour-old tracks can look brand new, but the deer may be over a half-mile away by that time and traveling faster than you.   It may be worth a try some days, but I think the percentages are better if you stick with your original plan.   In any event, test each step before you put full weight on that foot when there's snow on the ground or, better still, resort to the tactics, coming up next, for hunting in dry woods.

Bone-dry leaves provide one of the toughest conditions a still-hunter faces and one of the most common ones.   You need all the help you can get on days like this, and here are some tips to cut down on that fatal crunch-crunch.   Try to walk under evergreens just back from the hardwoods wherever conditions permit.   This is good tactic at all times since you're harder to see under that poorer light, but there's an even more compelling reason on dry days.   Pine and hemlock needles are quiet underfoot even when leaves sound like saltines.   Roots, rocks, and logs are noise-free, too.   You'll find the most rocks below ledges and cliffs.   They've fallen off the formations above.   And there are more exposed roots on steep slopes where erosion has bared them.   Edges of hemlock swamps are excellent, too, for these shallow-rooted trees often send out large, exposed roots many feet from their trunks.

Look for these same noise-reducers when there's crusty snow, too, because this situation is as bad as dry leaves, or maybe worse.   But there's one ace in the hole that lets you beat both conditions when the chips are down and all else fails—*being properly equipped*.

Those rather uncomfortable and bulky rubber boots I mentioned earlier are my secret weapon here.   No matter how dry the leaves or crunchy the snow, I can walk up small creeks and trickles and through the soppy parts of hemlock swamps without making a sound and in perfect comfort with this footwear.   Meanwhile, any deer that so much as moves a foot within a couple of hundred yards gives himself away.

When you can't find shallow water to hide your sounds, there's still hope even under the worst conditions.   Walk just above a major rise or ledge as you cut cross-contour.   Deer may hear you and freeze, but the sound comes to them indirectly and they can't locate your exact position.   Pussyfoot down to a look-out point every 200 feet or so during your

A proficient still-hunter acquires a keen eye for sign (in this case a buck rub on a white cedar). He may take hours to get through a small patch of cover and browse, watching, listening, and making new decisions about his maneuvers on the basis of his observations. Often, he will combine still- and stand-hunting. (Photo: Norm Nelson)

Many Eastern sportsmen have the notion that still-hunting is an effective technique only for whitetails—that mule deer are taken by cruising in an off-road vehicle or by horseback, stopping frequently to glass the terrain. Actually, these and other techniques work well under the right conditions. In cover like this, with a few inches of snow on the ground, a lot of excellent muley trophies are garnered by still-hunting. Few of us would pass up a buck like the one pictured. (Photo: Russell Tinsley)

traverse and spend several minutes glassing the flat below. Take your time. The deer will probably be frozen, as I've said, and they're hard to pick out, but don't move on until you're absolutely certain there are none in sight. There's a special satisfaction in catching even a doe with her guard down when you're hunting like this, though it doesn't give you a shot. It means you've executed the maneuver perfectly and you can take pride in counting a *coup* the way Indian warriors sometimes used to hit their enemies with a lancelike stick rather than killing and scalping them.

Not only does still-hunting give you the greatest joys of accomplishment, I'm convinced it allows the greatest flexibility, too. So far I've talked only of hunting solo which is the most satisfying of all to me personally. But two or several hunters can still-hunt a woods simultaneously if there's enough elbow room. If they travel roughly parallel to each other a few hundred yards apart, they may even increase their chances by pushing the wariest, unseen deer toward each other.

After the best of the morning is over, they can assemble at a prearranged place and set up informal drives through dense bed-down territory with one or two of them acting as standers. Then they can still-hunt downhill separately in late afternoon and take stationary positions near orchards and fields during those last productive minutes of shooting light. With a good knowledge of the territory, an understanding of the habits of the local deer herd plus a little imagination, a group of knowledgeable still-hunters can make good and productive use of all the legal shooting hours.

Then, too, there's a humbling element about still-hunting that I find not exactly unpleasing. The more you hunt this way, the more you come to respect deer as far better woodsmen than you'll ever be. Even under the best conditions, most deer will drift out ahead of you without your ever seeing or hearing them. And it will be a rare day when you scope more deer than you see tails bounding off out of sight.

But, as I've said, this is percentage hunting. Remember, bucks make mistakes, too. And sometimes vagaries of air or natural advantages of terrain can play into your hands.

Above all, don't let an occasional lucky success go to your head and lead you into sloppy habits. The better you know your territory, the more you use your head, the more you stare out beyond where you can really see, the slower and quieter you can make your way through the woods—the more venison steaks you'll enjoy.

3

The Secrets of Stand-Hunting

by Jim Carmichel

As a former Tennessee farm lad I suppose I'm a product of what's known as the Protestant work ethnic—that being the philosophy that nothing comes easy and those who are most successful in life are those who work hardest.

I didn't realize the impact this background was having on my mode of operation—and deer hunting in particular—until one crisp day a few years back when I crashed through a final ring of brush and topped out on a high mesa in northeastern New Mexico's high plains. A few moments later there was another crashing in the dry brush and a hunting companion, a fellow of upbringing similar to mine, came into the clearing and plopped down on the log where I was sitting. For a while we panted in silence, asking ourselves why we had struggled up the steepest hill in the territory while the rest of our hunting party circled the gentle landscape below.

Finally, when we'd both gotten our wind back, my friend said, "I just can't understand it. I do this every time I go deer hunting. Something in the back of my mind keeps telling me that if I work harder, push farther, and climb higher I'll be rewarded with a nice buck."

"But you know what?" he went on. "It has never worked out that way for me."

"I know exactly what you mean," I answered, "but from now on I'm going to start using my head instead of my feet."

That was my "conversion" to stand-hunting, and in the ensuing years I've managed to take more deer, walk less miles, suffer fewer sore muscles, and have more fun deer hunting than I would ever have guessed in earlier times.

By popular definition, "stand-hunting" is taking a fixed position in a tree or relatively concealed spot on the ground and waiting for a deer to come by. This is not to be confused with still-hunting, which is the art of making a cautious stop-and-go circuit through deer country. "Stalking," by comparison, is a fairly steady gait.

41

A Texas hunter watches the brush and the openings from an improvised tree stand. He has a good wide view and room to swing his rifle. In addition, he's out of sight, and he would be concealed well even if the foliage didn't obscure him because deer don't look up much. He's also above the plane of scent. There are many regions where such a stand can produce muley as well as whitetail venison. (Photo: Russell Tinsley)

Actually the art and technique of stand-hunting is widely misunderstood and just as often misapplied. It is most especially misunderstood by overeager hunters who don't feel they've truly gotten their license-money's worth until they've bounded over every inch of the hunting territory. This, quite frankly, was me in my younger days. Likewise, I also tended to share the opinion that stand-hunters were just too lazy or uninterested to go after deer in proper fashion. It always seemed to me that the odds were against the stand-hunter. After all, I reasoned, there were few deer to start with, they were scattered over a wide area, and the chances of a deer coming by any particular spot were extremely remote.

Actually, almost the exact opposite is true. There are more deer in most areas than the average moving hunter will ever realize; they are not scattered over a wide area but, rather, tend to concentrate in certain pockets; and the chances of a given deer passing by a certain spot every day are almost as good as the chances that you regularly pass a given spot on your way to work each day!

"Ah," you say, "but there's the rub. How do you know that magic spot where a deer will pass?"

The late dean of hunting authors, Larry Koller, proves that an on-the-ground stand—nothing fancy, no constructed blind—can produce if the hunter's outline is broken or concealed, if the wind is right, and if the location commands a view of a crossing or deer run.

That, dear deer hunter, is precisely the skill of stand-hunting. In fact, it's more than just a skill. When done correctly, it's a science—the science of understanding deer habits, knowing when they move, where they move, and why they move. In recent years the more successful stand-hunters have also taken into consideration the added dimension of hunter movements. But more about this later. First let's examine the stand.

A deer stand can be anything from a stump to a cozy box on top of a steel tower. It should conceal the hunter but at the same time allow him clear vision over the surrounding area and permit safe and accurate shooting. This latter should never be forgotten or underestimated. Probably the worst example of this I've ever seen was a stand I once tried to use on the edge of a swamp in Africa. I was hunting the sitatunga, a little swamp-dwelling antelope that spends most of its time hidden in reeds and .bulrushes and seldom ventures out into an open area. When it does, the range is often several hundred yards. Usually the only possible way to spot these shy creatures is from a perch in a high tree. Accordingly, my guide rigged a perch so high in a tree that it was necessary to hold on with both hands to keep from falling out! Any possibility of holding and aiming a rifle was out of the question.

The same thing sometimes happens to deer hunters who spend great time and effort in climbing a tree or mounting a perch only to find that their position prevents them from making a well-aimed shot.

Every year we read about hunters who break an arm or leg by falling out of a tree. For those who cannot climb as agilely as a squirrel or perch on a limb as lightly as a bird, the portable tree stand and "self-climbing" platform can be, literally, a lifesaver. Several types are available, and regardless of differences in design they're all intended to perch you up there efficiently and safely. (For information on a couple of approaches to this problem, you can write to Baker's Tree Stands, Box 1003, Valdosta, Georgia 31601, and Hunter's Hideout Tree Stand Co., 1817 McKeon Road, Kenosha, Wisconsin 53140.)

I personally prefer a stand that is up in a tree or at least elevated enough to give a wide view. I'm of the opinion that deer have more difficulty picking up a hunter's scent if he is somewhat elevated, although I know some experienced hunters who are of a different mind.

Surprisingly, perhaps, the stand does not need to be especially well camouflaged or for that matter, camouflaged at all. Once in Europe and again in South Carolina I hunted from a stand that was nothing more than a simple 4×4-foot plywood box on top of a 12-foot metal tower. Naturally, if you erect such a stand on the first day of deer season there is about as much chance of a buck stopping by as there is of holding the Southern Baptist Convention at the Vatican. The trick is to establish your blind well ahead of the hunting season so that the deer in the area will become accustomed to the structure and accept it as a normal, harmless part of their environment. Three months ahead of the season opening is none too soon.

Also, don't set up some sort of eyesore contraption that will offend the landowner, state or federal authorities (if you hunt on public land), and other hunters. And, of course, check the local and state regulations. Such a structure is legal in most regions, but you can't take that for granted. The building of a permanent structure, in particular, is prohibited on some lands. Finally, to prevent off-season vandalism or the unauthorized use of your blind, it should be concealed so as to hide it from other people throughout the year.

An effective ground-level stand can be made by piling up slash from logging operations or whatever natural growth may be at hand. Remember, though, if you cut brush during the summer the green leaves will dry and fall off and leave a pretty sorry-looking blind. So plan ahead and "think winter." Oak is a good choice for blind material because the dead leaves hold pretty fast, and of course evergreens will stay dense. I advise making several openings for spotting and shooting rather than just looking over the top of a brush blind. If you have to stand up and shoot over the top of a blind, your movement will spook a buck before you can get a shot off.   It may be a great thrill to pull off a shot at a bounding buck, but the averages are all in favor of the hunter who has a standing or slowly moving target.

A little while back I said that a stand can be just about anything, including a stump.   It bears repetition here that a stand, to be good, doesn't always have to be a man-made platform or artificial blind.   Often the best blind is provided by the terrain or vegetation near a deer run, crossing, or other choice location.   In other words, an excellent stand may simply consist of a position that gives you a good view where deer traffic can be expected, and at the same time either hides you or breaks up your outline sufficiently so that a buck won't spot you before you spot him.   You also want to be as careful as conditions permit that your scent won't spook him, and I'll go into that in a moment.

The point I'm making here is that an effective blind may be a blow-down, a little shrubbery thicket, the crotch of a sufficiently large tree, even a rock outcropping or cliff.   Bob Elman, the editor of this book, tells me that for two years in a row he's had a 30- to 40-yard shot at a browsing whitetail from atop a 6-foot boulder on a beech ridge in the Catskills. The boulder overlooks a heavily used deer trail between daytime bedding grounds and some abandoned orchards where the whitetails love to feed at night.   The prevailing early-morning breeze flows up the ridge toward him, so it doesn't carry his scent to the game.   From his boulder he can look down on any passing deer, but they seldom look up at him.

Properly locating a deer stand is far more complex than just strolling out in the woods and setting up shop in a "likely looking" spot.   This is where careful preseason scouting pays big dividends.   As you scout an area, you'll find that the local herd tends to follow well-used trails.   During a buck's daily activity he will feed, water, and bed down according to a regular schedule.   More important, from the hunter's standpoint, is the fact that the buck will tend to follow a specific route as he attends to these daily activities.   The preseason scouter who discovers these routes will be able to take up a stand where he knows there is regular deer traffic.

If you intend to hunt from a "natural" stand such as downed timber, slash piles, etc., you are flexible enough to adapt to prevailing wind conditions on any given day.   However, if you intend to establish a permanent blind, you'll be smart to take into account annual prevailing wind conditions and locate yourself accordingly.

To us humans the scenting of other animals over a distance of several hundred yards is only an abstraction.   We believe it because we've been told it's true but we still tend to regard it as a rather ghostly supposition.   But to a deer, a hunter's scent is as real as seeing or touching him and just as good a cause for running the other way.   You wouldn't stand up, wave your arms, and shout at a deer, and neither should you get located where he is sure to catch your scent.

If you scout an area during the last few days before the season opens, be on the lookout for deer rubs and scrapes. When the velvet on a buck's antlers dries, he rubs it off on slender trees. This tears the bark and some of the limbs off and is usually easy to spot. Areas that show lots of rub sign are natural areas to look for bucks and are good places for stand-hunting. "Scrapes," or "kicks," are even better. These are spots where a buck cleans the ground and leaves his scent to attract females. He will visit these scrapes periodically to see if he has "caught" any

Commercial stands are deservedly popular, because a hunter can't always find a properly located tree with a comfortably stout and safe limb—or enough low branches to make it climbable. This rifleman is up high enough so he needn't worry about concealment. (Photo: Baker Manufacturing Co.)

Here's a Baker Tree Climber in operation. This "self-climbing" stand not only provides an elevated seat once the hunter ascends the tree; it also gives him a tool that enables him to do the climbing quickly, safely, and with relative ease, hoisting himself up somewhat like a telephone lineman. (Photo: Baker Manufacturing Co.)

does. Don't locate your stand right on top of these ''baited'' spots but only close enough to have a reasonably clear view.

One of the smartest things a deer hunter can do, even if he only gets to do it once in his hunting career, is to get into the hunting area a few days before the season opens—the last couple of days are no good because of too much human activity—and study deer movements from dawn until dark. This experience quite often completely changes the hunter's perspective and makes him far more effective in his technique.

I know individuals who confessed utter amazement at the number of deer they saw just by sitting still in one place for the day. And, too, it can

This is the Hunter Hideout tree stand. It's simple and compact but also secure—the chain and the leverage of the seat itself will hold it against the tree trunk with great stability. And a seat like this is a lot more comfortable than a narrow limb.

be a delightfully pleasant day. Take your camera along and you can amaze your buddies with the ''shots'' at deer you'll get. One of the things you'll be most impressed by is the relatively high activity at first and last light of day. On an average, you'll see at least as many deer during the first and last half-hours of the day as the rest of the day in total. The value of this observation is that from then on you'll be at your stand before daylight.

Another lesson worth learning is that bucks tend to be considerably more wary than does of suspicious-looking situations. Some years back, when I was testing the relative effect on deer of different types and colors of camouflage hunting gear, I noted that so long as I remained perfectly still and more or less blended with the background, does would come amazingly close without showing alarm or even concern. Once, within three hours, I had no less than eleven does browse by within 50 yards, even though I was completely visible from the soles of my boots to the button on top of my cap. But at no time during a three-day period did a buck come within sight! I'm convinced they spotted me from a distance and decided that all was not as it should be. However, bucks will come close if the hunter is well hidden in a stand. This is why successful stand-hunting calls for a fair degree of thought and preparation.

Such thought and preparation can include a few fancy touches that increase your chances of connecting. So far we've been talking about the science of hunting from a stand—proven facts and techniques that get results. But the real experts go a step farther and apply the art of stand-hunting.

If you hunt in an area where there are few other hunters, you will undoubtedly be most successful by playing the odds and using a stand near established and known deer-traffic areas. But with more and more hunters taking to the fields and forests every season, the day has all but passed when you can reasonably assume you're the only person in the woods with a gun.

Most hunters dislike this competition but a smart stand-hunter can make good use of the other hunters. The presence of a few hunters in an area does not seem to seriously affect a deer's daily regime. However, when a lot of hunters are in an area, the animals will alter their habits drastically. Consider a case in point:

Let's say a local herd of deer is in the habit of feeding in a low meadow during the predawn hours and then, just at sunup, they normally circle clockwise around a low hill, move into a valley between two higher hills, and disperse into their favorite bedding areas on the lower slopes.

But on the opening morning of deer season, dozens of hunters move into the area and disturb the normal routine. Even though the deer's usual habits have been aborted, they will follow a more or less predictable pattern. The smart hunter knows this and will take advantage of the situation while his less astute fellow hunters are wondering where all the deer went.

First of all, keep in mind that deer are creatures of habit. If a buck likes to bed down during the day at a certain spot, he is not likely to give up that spot simply because his normal route is blocked. Instead, he will get there by the back door. If hunting pressure is really intense, he may decide to leave the area altogether, but in either case he will follow a route that is familiar.

The observant preseason scouter will have made note of little-used game trails which generally lead to the same location as the more heavily used trails.

These are escape routes which are used throughout the year whenever dogs, lumbermen, hikers, campers, etc., disrupt the daily habits of the deer. During the hunting season, these routes frequently become the principally used deer highways. Thus the above-mentioned deer, which normally move clockwise around a low hill, may suddenly find that they must go over the hill or possibly circle it in the opposite direction in order to reach their customary bedding area.

Usually deer will have several such routes but it's a good bet they will select the one that heads them into the wind on that particular day. So

This buck is alerted. He's winded the hunter-photographer, and in another moment he'll see him and perhaps hear him, as well. But then it will be too late. A well-chosen stand frequently results in this kind of close-range, broadside target.

the smart hunter who knows the various possible routes can also take up a stand on the path most likely to be used that day.

In fact, a clever hunter can sometimes even determine which way the deer will travel before they know themselves. If there is a road or popular camping site near the hunting area, it's a good guess that a high percentage of the hunters will be entering the woods from that direction. This means the deer will be driven in the opposite direction.

By taking this into consideration, plus investigating the possible routes the retreating deer will take, you can be at your stand, ready and waiting, when that big buck comes by.

4

The When, Where, and How of Deer-Driving

by Robert Elman

In the previous chapter, Jim Carmichel observed that a lot more deer can be taken by stand-hunting than by still-hunting. Jim is a nationally respected writer—and besides, the truth of his observation is obvious. In Chapter 2, Len Wright says he'd rather still-hunt because it's more interesting to move around (warmer, too) and often more challenging; or at least it demands more frequent decisions based on deer craft as the hunter moves along. He even figures that after a light snow it may be at least as productive as stand-hunting. I've spent many days in the woods with Len and can attest to his knowledge of the game.

It would seem, then, that I might well concentrate on stand-hunting or still-hunting or a combination of the two, not only in my hunting but in my writing about it.

Yet here I am, pounding an elderly and defenseless typewriter in praise of deer-driving, a method actually scorned as vulgar by a few of the more snobbish latter-day "Leather-Stockings." Which may prompt the innocents who haven't had extensive experience with all three techniques to ask which of them really is best. At the risk of undermining my case, I won't just nominate deer-driving and let it go at that. Such an answer would be simplistic and misleading.

Driving accounts for more deer per hunting hour or day than either of the other two methods, and probably brings in a larger total harvest of venison. But since it requires teamwork by at least two hunters, and sometimes two dozen or two score, it doesn't necessarily take more deer per hunter. Which method is best? An answer is valid only in terms of some specific situation.

Let's say, for instance, that you want to hunt very thick cover where the brush won't give you many chances to see a deer at 40 yards, much less at 80 or 100. There are few or no spots here that combine the three requisites for a really good stand: signs of deer traffic within range; a wide, deep arc of visibility for the hunter; and a way for him to avoid being seen, heard, or winded by his game before he can get a shot.

Just to make it a classic situation, and one calling for a particular kind of drive, let's also say you're in a place where you can't use a rifle.   In New Jersey, to cite the usual example, for the sake of safety in woods rimmed by heavily populated areas the pre-1975 law called for buckshot or nothing.   Slugs have been permitted since opening day of 1975, but still no rifles; hence no shots at even moderately long range.   Stand- or still-hunting is apt to be chancy here.

Maybe the visibility will do at a couple of spots along the edges, but the wind is wrong or a farmhouse is too close or there's some other disadvantage.   So you decide against a stand.   As for still-hunting through these thickets, the weather has been so dry that every step sounds like popping corn, only louder.   During the first or last half-hour of shooting light, you might get stubborn and take a stand, but now it's midmorning and the deer aren't moving unless something pushes them.

They're invisible but you know they're in there.   You've seen tracks, droppings, buck rubs.   You've seen the ends of twigs nipped where they've browsed.   One recent evening, perhaps, you've even seen a good buck bound across a road at one edge.   There you have a situation that calls for a drive—a big, noisy drive.

I recall reading a description by some eminent expert—I think it was Warren Page—of a situation like that.   Most of my deer hunting had been with a rifle, and I thought he was exaggerating the density of the cover he'd encountered as well as the carnival atmosphere of a drive.   That's what I thought—until I was introduced to the "pineys" of lower New Jersey, where there are stretches best worked by the Old World technique involving beaters.   Once I joined seventeen other men to push several deer out of an extended thicket, and I'm told that some hunting clubs would have called that a small drive.

Half of us were standers.   We spread out along an old dirt road on the downwind end of the woods.   At one extreme of the line, three men moved forward a bit, along the edge of a fallow field, and three more at the other extreme moved forward up a wide power line right-of-way that intersected the road where the rest of us waited.   In other words, we didn't form a straight line but a rough U, because pushed deer will often sneak out to the sides, especially toward the end of a drive.

The other half of our team—nine more men—moved through the woods, beginning at a prearranged time, from the upwind end.   When you're serving as a driver, that's the one time in deer hunting when you may want the wind at your back.   You want the deer to scent you, because that will move them toward the standers.

A small, quiet drive is apt to give the standers (and sometimes the drivers) a shot at a deer moving about like this—not panicked and running full-out but just nervous, moving slowly enough to provide a shot for a carefully aimed rifle. (Photo: Illinois Dept. of Conservation)

Those nine drivers went through the woods at a moderate pace (no faster pace was possible in the thicker parts of the woods) but they made a hellish racket, hooting and calling. Artificial noisemakers aren't legal everywhere, but they are in New Jersey. One man even had an aluminum skillet he banged against the butt of his shotgun, and another had a loud dog whistle. When they were about 200 yards from us, they spread out to the sides for safety's sake, but three deer they'd been pushing came straight on. I should add that this drive had a captain, as every drive should, and—again for safety—his word was law. As another standard precaution, no stander budged from his assigned position, regardless of temptations.

The noise, the crowd, and the thickness of the cover reminded me of the club hunts with dogs in parts of the South, though that's distinctly different from a conventional drive, as you know if you've had the unique experience or have read the accounts of Tom Brakefield in the next chapter. This particular New Jersey drive was noisier than a Southern hunt with dogs. It wasn't what you'd call stylish, but I couldn't argue with the results even though I much prefer the other traditional driving method—the small, quiet drive.

With either strategy, drivers and standers take turns so that the hunt is fair to all if at least two drives are staged. Not that a driver never gets a shot. If the area being covered is big enough so that a driver can safely shoot during the early stages of the push, he may very well nail a deer. As a matter of fact, doubling back and trying to sneak out between the drivers is a frequent trick of deer, particularly mature (which means smart) bucks. And not only bucks. On a recent West Virginia grouse hunt, of

This spike buck is a bounding, difficult target—the typical product of a big, noisy drive. But where the cover is dense such a drive may be the only way to get any shots at all. And where shotguns are used and the range is apt to be very short, a picture like this is what the hunter expects—and hopes for. (Photo: Leonard Lee Rue III)

all things, I was almost knocked down by a doe when I unwittingly pushed her up a ridge into a very steep, thick tangle that she didn't like the looks of. She panicked, wheeled, came straight back at me, and bounded out right over my head.

To counter this backtracking habit of deer, the most effective drives employ what my friends and I call "backstops"—a few hunters who follow the drivers, straggling a good distance behind them to intercept game that insists on heading the wrong way. This is most important in hunting whitetails, but it's also good insurance when driving mule deer through some thicket or canyon. And perhaps it's most important not on the big, noisy drives but on the small, quiet type for which I've expressed a preference.

Now let's examine that more restrained style of driving. The first point to make is that it's much more effective than the noisy stampede if rifles can be used, if the woods aren't quite so dense, and if there are openings or stretches of clear or open terrain such as fields at the terminus of the drive.

A fast, noisy invasion by the hordes of Genghis Khan will spook more deer into doubling back or sneaking out to the sides, and will panic many into a flat-out, straight-ahead run. Even with buckshot, I have reservations about shooting at a fast-running deer. Most of my venison has been collected by squeezing off careful rifle shots at deer that were pausing uncertainly, walking, or trotting more or less slowly. That's how deer generally move when they're just being gently driven from their browsing or bedding areas—when all they detect is a distant, unwelcome intrusion from which they can cautiously edge away, often in so leisurely a manner that they go right on browsing as they move unsuspectingly toward the standers.

There are classic situations that call for this kind of drive, too.   Last season, in the Pennsylvania Gamelands, I discovered a piece of habitat that's perfect for a small drive and has to be one of the country's game-richest pockets of land open to public hunting.   In my whitetailing experience, it is surpassed only by a privately owned principality known as the YO Ranch in Texas.   A few friends and I plan to drive the same Pennsylvania pocket next year.   I have no intention of disclosing its location.   I'm not one of those kiss-and-tell writers who encourage their readers to converge on a so-called "hotspot" and hunt it barren.   I found this one; you can find your own.   But I will explain why this particular area is so ripe for a quiet drive.

It's a narrow, very boggy, thickly brushed island no more than a quarter of a mile long and only a few yards from the shore of a big, deep lake.   One end is just flat, open bog, so the whole quarter-mile doesn't have to be driven.   On one side of the island the lake keeps the deer from sneaking off to evade hunters.   On the other side, between the island and high, dry ground, there's a thin stretch of swamp that can't be crossed by hunters without hip boots or waders.   Beyond the swamp is a rise of woods, open enough to shoot through.

Driving is not a method limited to the East or to whitetail cover.   In many parts of the West, the kind of muley drive described by the author can push bucks into the open in front of a shooter, as shown here.   (Photo: Montana Chamber of Commerce)

Beginning half an hour before sunrise on opening day, the adjacent timber is suddenly festooned with red- and orange-clad riflemen, popping out everywhere like desert blossoms after a rain. Not wishing to invade the privacy of these gentlemen, most of the deer head for brushy thickets on the highest, farthest ridges. That's what they're supposed to do, as all of us have read in scores of books and articles. But many are turned back by the scent, sound, and sight of all those gun-toting wolves in Santa's clothing. They must look elsewhere for refuge. The deer, after all, make the rules and, when frustrated, feel free to break the rules. The swamp is a barrier to the hunters but not to the deer, and you wouldn't believe how many whitetails I think must crowd back onto that island. Except for my own group, I haven't yet seen any smart deer-stalkers using a canoe to get onto the island from the lake side or donning waders to reach it through the swamp.

During the first hour or so of legal shooting time, the best bet is to stay off the island and take a high stand on the ridge overlooking the swamp. Deer have been browsing down there, and they'll be moving up to drier, normally undisturbed bedding thickets. If the ground is wet or snow-blanketed, there's nothing to prevent still-hunting along the landward edge of the swamp for a little while after that first hour or so. Some of the spooked deer are now returning, and a hunter can keep pretty much out of sight as he moves along that edge. However, there's the possibility that a buck will hear or wind anyone moving and will shy away, so a better idea is to switch from the traditional stand, high on the ridge, to a lowland stand in a tree or one of the blowdowns near the game trails entering the swamp. A buck can be intercepted there as he retreats toward the island.

By midmorning, however, plenty of deer have safely made it to the island and aren't planning to leave before dusk. Now it's time for two or three men to drive that island's brushy portion from one end to the other, while three men wait on the landward side, above the swamp, and one or two more stand guard on a shoreline bluff at the far end. The standers must be in position before the drivers even begin their approach to the island, of course, or the deer will skulk their way out. Whether the drivers reach the island from the swamp side, wearing waders, or by boat or canoe from the lake side, once they've arrived the deer can avoid them only by passing the standers. The island is narrow enough to require just two or three drivers, and though it's brushy there are openings. One of the drivers may well get a shot if everyone moves slowly and quietly. And if no bucks provide shots on the island, they'll be targets for the standers as they make their way up out of the shoreside swamp and through the open woods.

On opening day, I found that ideal spot accidentally, while still-hunting with a female partner. Little Red Riding Hood and I bumped a pair of does, failed to wait long enough to see if a buck was trailing them—and when he finally arrived our noisy walking sent him crashing and splashing back into the island's concealing brush before either of us could get a scope on him. The next day I was alone, equipped with hip boots, and determined to hunt the island itself. However, while in the swamp water I managed to step into a beaver hole. I lost my balance and my eyeglasses (which, as it happened, did not float), filled my boots with enough water to lower the swamp level, washed my hat, and got out of the woods just as my clothing was freezing stiff enough to make me creak like the Tin Woodsman. (Outdoor writers aren't supposed to confess all these blunders, but whom are we kidding?)

On the same day, two members of my party took stands near there. One of them missed a spike buck running out of the swamp and the other, cramped by cold, was a trifle too slow to get his scope on an eight-pointer sneaking back in. I had to go home that night, but before I left I suggested the kind of drive I've just described. A couple of days later one of my friends phoned to acknowledge my cleverness (if not my agility around beaver holes) and offer me a roast from the venison he'd harvested.

There are many other kinds of habitat pockets almost as nicely suited to a small, quiet drive. Generally speaking, I'd say such a drive ought to cover no larger an area than a square mile—usually much less—or it will be spread too thin to be effective. Depending on the terrain, the cover, and the number of participants you can round up, the ideal operation usually involves half a dozen to a dozen men.

With half of them standing and half of them driving, they can comb such promising spots as woodlots ending in open terrain, crossings between browse and bedding ridges, timber or brush cut by power line rights-of-way or old logging and farm roads, swamps, notches, and saddles, or brushy gullies where standers can be ready on the rims and at one end.

I've heard about dead-end canyons where quiet drivers can corner a mule deer without the aid of standers. Admittedly, I've hunted mule deer only in Texas (and only in two parts of Texas, at that) so I certainly can't say dead-end canyons don't exist. But I've never seen one where a muley couldn't sneak back or top out while the hunters were pushing through scrub and rubble that might keep them from spotting the game. A drive without standers isn't a true drive but a still-hunt and should be conducted accordingly. It is, however, a team effort and, for efficiency and safety, ought to be captained like an Eastern whitetail drive and ought to follow at least a rough prearranged pattern. It does work well in some canyons, and it works perhaps even better on big wooded flats where the drivers just keep moving the deer about for one another.

In parts of the South, particularly where the cover is thick and tangled, drives (with or without dogs) tend to be big social affairs. They also tend to be productive, as proved by this photo of seven Tennessee hunters with seven nice bucks. (Photo: Tennessee Game & Fish Commission)

Since quiet drives of moderate size are also productive in some of the Western mountains and bottomland prairie thickets, I don't understand why most hunters seem to forget that muleys can be driven like whitetails. Drives work well in wooded basins, the thickets around streams, and the open-bordered groves of mixed shelter and browse such as aspen and oak or conifers. As I've mentioned in other writings, where ridges or draws (or both) cut through such cover as cedar and piñon woods, you have another good variation on the theme. I've seen muleys as well as whitetails herded slowly out of the cover, up onto more open ridges or down into the draws to streams where a rifleman can often get a good, clear shot.

East or West, for whitetails or mule deer, there's yet another ideal setup for a drive, particularly on dry, crackly mornings when still-hunting is too noisy or when the wind keeps shifting and there's no really good spot for a lone hunter to take a stand. I'm referring to any reasonably open deer-crossing between feeding areas and bedding grounds. Before daybreak, standers selected by the captain sweep around onto the high bedding grounds—heading in from the flanks and the far side to avoid prematurely pushing deer up ahead of them. Then they move down somewhat and settle themselves at the forest edge where they can see into the crossing. At a prearranged time, when the standers should be in position, the drivers begin still-hunting up from the nocturnal browsing area onto the crossing.

On the basis of my own experience, I'd say it's wisest not to walk straight out over the crossing, directly toward the higher woods. The standers are waiting at the fringes of those woods, hidden or with their outlines broken by brush, rocks, and timber. They're hoping to get shots at deer in the relatively open crossing. The drivers move along this crossing, obliquely toward the standers. The expectation is that game will be sighted before the drivers are opposite the standers. Members of either group may then be presented with shots that won't endanger anyone. And deer that are pushed laterally along a crossing will tend to flank out toward higher woods—toward the standers.

I've been describing an early-morning drive, of course. If your party keeps hunting through midday, the areas to be driven are usually the high ridges rather than the crossings, but standers at the crossings will have a chance at game driven off those ridges. And late in the day, the morning procedure is simply reversed to intercept deer coming down from bedding to browsing areas.

A point should be made here regarding the emphasis I've put on openings, cuts, borders, crossings, and the like. By no means is it always mandatory that standers be positioned along some kind of clearing. Often, particularly in hilly or mountainous regions, you won't find a field or orchard or wide open road or even a strategically located clearing, but you will find patches of woods that narrow to a neck—between hills, bluffs, watercourses, or perhaps sheer cliffs if you're lucky. Standers positioned above a neck, on each side, will often get a clear view down into it in spite of woods or brush. And a quiet drive can herd the bucks into that neck. In a narrow patch of woods, even a two-man drive may work: one man waits above while the other quietly hunts through the timber, prodding deer far ahead of him toward the neck.

Two men can also work a ridgeline quite well. One of them stays on the crest while the other moves along slowly and quietly a couple of hundred yards below. Or two men can flank a deer trail, so that either of them is likely to spook a buck out across the other man's front. A trio is more efficient on a miniature trail drive, though. The third man stays

Elman poses with a Texas whitetail he killed after a brief three-man drive. His two partners nudged the buck and a pair of does out of a thicket—gently and quietly—while the author waited on stand. The buck wanted to hang back but reluctantly followed the does into the crossing as the two drivers made their approach.

A successful drive can be made by just two partners working a ridge, a saddle, a neck, or a deer trail. In this case they worked a trail, and the buck, moving away from the scent and sound of one hunter, swung around right in front of the other.

more or less on the deer run. Regardless of whether a buck moving ahead of him turns out to the right or left, a hunter may intercept him. Still another variation—one I've observed in the West—is pebble-tossing, sometimes with the aid of a slingshot. Suppose a brushy ravine is to be driven, and there are only two men to do it. They move along the two rims, tossing stones down into the scrub so that what a buck hears is noise down where he is. That's likely to prod him out of the shielding cover, up one side of the ravine or the other. In the Big Bend country, a friend and I once "rocked" a buck mule deer out of a coulee onto a bald flat that way.

I've seen deer-driving treatises illustrated with pseudo-scientific diagrams featuring arrows and numbers and reassuringly technical-looking symbols designating drivers, backstops, end-standers, flank-standers, and even the deer themselves. I would never bad-mouth such meticulously drafted maps, but neither would I ever hope to find a piece of hunting country and a local deer population considerate enough to precisely match those diagrams. Seldom have I even had available the exact number of hunters called for by the printed symbols. Deer-driving is not a science. It is a fairly simple art whose suitability and probable success depend on local terrain and cover, recent hunting pressure, the weather, the feeding and bedding habits of the deer (and of the hunters if they're more inclined to sleep late and eat big than to climb early and shiver long)—and perhaps a few other variable factors that don't come to mind until they actually help or hinder the whole business.

For anyone who feels in need of advice, mine is to forget the diagrams in the literature and concentrate on the general rules of thumb I've stressed: a size and style of drive suited to the immediate situation, a safe and never whimsically altered plan for both drivers and standers, the use of flankers almost always and backstops when possible, and a thorough knowledge of local deer haunts and habits as well as advantageous features of topography and vegetation. At my deer camp last fall, someone spoke of acquiring "deer-driving sense." What he meant was horse sense.

5

The Sporting Use of Dogs

by Tom Brakefield

I was damp and cold, and after more than an hour motionless on the deer stand my teeth were beginning to chatter like castanets. I'd forgotten how cold southern Alabama can get during the January monsoon season. Then I heard the dogs baying for the first time. Were they getting closer or had the wind just shifted so that it was funneling the sound my way more efficiently? No, definitely getting closer now. I tensed as the dogs drew still nearer. Apparently they were coming directly toward me. I rolled my eyes from side to side, straining to take in as much territory as possible because I realized that the deer would probably be some 300 to 400 yards ahead of the dogs and not necessarily directly in front of them.

I clamped my jaws shut to stop the chattering which had graduated from the castanet class to the pneumatic-drill category. Tentatively I flexed my muscles, wondering if I could get them to work right after the long numbing period of stillness. Sharp needles pierced the soles of each foot but my backsides were an unfeeling block of granite.

Then the dogs veered off and their baying muted as they headed away from me. However, I continued to strain my eyes as I looked at, and tried to look through, the terrifically thick cover all around me. Just because the dogs were moving away didn't mean I was out of the ball game. They could be on a loop of deer scent while the deer, especially if he was a wily old-timer with a trophy rack, could be skulking back my way. That kind of sustained excitement is one of the bonuses of this greatly misunderstood way of hunting deer. Finally, after 15 minutes, I sighed and stretched, feeling like Rip van Winkle unwrapping from his 20 years in the sack. The deer had headed the other way, or if he had come by my stand I hadn't seen him. Either way he was long gone by now.

That evening while I luxuriated under a hot shower I pondered about how misunderstood, throughout most of the country, hunting deer with dogs is. This is really quite surprising when you consider that the prac-

Members of a Southern club gather in front of the camp while the huntmaster repeats the rules for any newcomers—no one strays from a stand, no one moves or talks while on stand, no one shoots unless he can see antlers, and so on. A Southern hunt with dogs is apt to be very well organized, and very quiet until the dogs arrive in the vicinity of the standers, moving deer ahead but not panicking them into a terrified run. (Photo: Tom Brakefield)

tice goes back to Colonial times in the South, that it is not unknown (in varying versions) in other parts of North America, and that it was a favored European method for centuries before the Colonists brought it to this country.

Hunters in various parts of eastern Canada regularly use dogs to trail wounded deer and moose. This is a wise and humane custom since it drastically reduces the amount of lost game. Even when a blood trail is present, it's occasionally possible for a wounded deer to elude a hunter—and any true sportsman is repelled by the thought of game dying slowly and being wasted. With dogs to do the trailing when the shot fails to bring a quick kill, this is unlikely. Dogs have also been used, at various times, in both Canada and Europe to flush out and course big game. This, too, is quite sporting when done properly and under appropriate circumstances. The uninitiated may have visions of a panic-stricken, exhausted deer stumbling past a hunter's stand just ahead of a pack of wild-eyed, bloody-fanged dogs, but it just doesn't work that way.

The real hotbed area for hunting deer with dogs lies in the Southeastern United States. Take a look at a map of that region. If you draw a line east-west across the states of Georgia, Alabama, and Mississippi, running somewhere between Montgomery and Tuscaloosa, Alabama, you will have the northern boundary of this area, which is fantastically rich (in both deer and thick cover). Another, much shorter, east-west line across the

In any dog hunt involving a large group of men, some stands will inevitably be more desirable than others because they're at frequently used trails or crossings. To ensure fair stand assignments at this Alabama camp, numbered tags are kept on nails along the wall over the mantel. The tags are tossed into a hat for a random drawing that will decide who stands where. Sooner or later, every hunter is apt to draw one of the better locations. (Photo: Tom Brakefield)

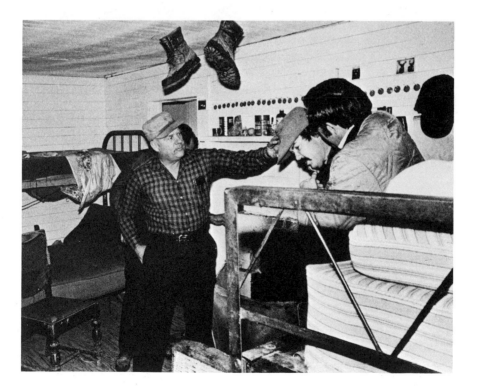

waist of Florida so that only the northern or panhandle section of that state is included, marks the southern limit of the dog-hunting area. Dogs may be used elsewhere, especially in various pockets of the general area surrounding this region, but this is far and away the primary area where the sport is still practiced regularly.

There are several reasons why it makes good sense to use dogs to run deer here. The Northern sportsman, used to hunting in thinner cover with much denser hordes of fellow hunters at his elbow, usually conjures up that nightmare picture I mentioned: a ravenous pack of dogs snapping at the very heels of the deer and finally running the poor exhausted creature to earth. The picture is reinforced by the unarguable fact that dogs can, if allowed to run loose and revert to a feral state, wreak enormous havoc on a deer herd over a period of time—especially when the deer are overcrowded, winter-weakened, or otherwise particularly vulnerable. But this is a far cry from the controlled use of dogs (and the right kind of dogs, as we shall see in a moment) to run deer in the South.

One of the reasons why dogs are used in this region is the cover. It's so thick, even in the winter, in this sub-tropical area that a Wisconsin or Pennsylvania deer hunter would be astonished. While it's true that a canny old whitetail buck can ghost his way unseen across a field with only the barest of cover, in this jungle of hanging vines and creepers (many studded with ultra-sharp heavy-duty prickers) and densely foliaged pines, a deer can often pass within 20 feet of a hunter unseen. In fact, another hunter, clad in red or orange, is usually spotted only at the last moment in these thickets. Still-hunting or driving in the conventional way is not only ineffective but out of the question in some of these tangles.

And there simply aren't enough hunters out, relative to the amount of deer, ground area, and cover, to stir things up enough like the massed infantry maneuvers that now pass for opening day in most of the "big" Eastern and Midwestern deer states. Without the dogs, the deer simply would not move around or be seen and harvested at anything like an adequate rate.

Even with the dogs it's doubtful that the deer are adequately harvested in many areas of this marvelously deer-rich region. Consider this: Alabama now has a herd of something over 500,000 deer, or about 10 per square mile statewide, including downtown Birmingham, Montgomery, and Mobile. In recent years the season has stretched for a long three months and the limit has been no more than one buck per day! Probably two-thirds of this immense herd is shoehorned into the lower half of the state where the dogs are used to run deer. Florida has some 450,000 deer, Mississippi has 400,000, and Georgia has 150,000 to 200,000, so these states aren't exactly slouches in the deer department, either. In fact, it's quite plain that all of these states but Georgia compare with or even outstrip many of the better-publicized "big" deer states of the East, Midwest, and West—in both herd density and total herd size.

If you have never hunted this thinly populated and thickly covered area, take my word for it that flushing out and killing deer without dogs would be extremely difficult, to say the least. In fact, to dispel the notion that with dogs the deer "don't have a chance," hunter success ratios hover around 20 to 30 percent in these states despite the tremendous deer densities, favorable hunter-to-deer ratios, and long seasons. Not exactly like potting fish in a barrel.

The preferred type of deer dog would surprise most hunters not familiar with this brand of hunting. They would probably visualize packs of hound dogs, no doubt led by bloodhounds. Nothing could be farther from reality! Deer dogs come in all shapes, shades, and sizes. All are mixed-breeds, usually with a touch (but only a touch) of hound in their checkered backgrounds. Actually, a good deer dog is one that is just

The huntmaster leads the long line of standers into the woods and drops them off, one by one, at their assigned locations before the dogs are started. (Photo: Tom Brakefield)

The hunter in this photo is only 20 feet from the camera lens, and he's in a relatively thin piece of cover. In woods like this, a deer is hard to see at 15 feet, and there's no way for a hunter to move around silently. This is why dog drives are considered a must in some parts of the South. (Photo: Tom Brakefield)

about worthless for anything else. You don't want the dog to be too cold-nosed or he'll spend excessive time trying to unravel a single deer trail that is hours old instead of moving on until he encounters a fresh trail. Nor do you want a fast dog. If he's too fast, he'll push a deer too hard and run him right out of the country with none of the standers getting a shot in the process. You don't want him to be too energetic or persistent or he may spend too much time on a trail that's less than smoking-hot. The idea is to stir things up.

There's really no training involved. If a dog will run anything, he'll run a deer, and all that's necessary to break a new dog in is to let him run in a pack with some older, experienced deer dogs. What the knowledgeable hunters want is a dog that will range out 200 or 300 yards in front of the dog drivers and handlers until he strikes a hot trail. Then he should work the trail slowly enough so that the deer will dawdle along some 300 to 500 yards in front of the dogs and keep looping through the same territory (where all the standers are spotted), never even leaving his home ground. One of the best deer dogs I've ever seen was a combination of basset hound and several other breeds. He was slow and had, at best, a so-so nose. He never ran a deer out of the country.

The dogs hardly ever catch up with a deer. If one of them does, there's either something wrong with that deer or the hunters will never run that dog again for deer. The idea is to maneuver the deer past as many hunters as possible, not to run the deer down. If the dog is speedy enough and aggressive enough to do that, he's not welcome in a Southern deer camp.

In a classic Southern deer-with-dogs hunt, there are usually two races a day, the morning run going out at around nine o'clock and lasting for two or maybe two and a half hours, and the afternoon run starting about three o'clock and lasting the same length of time. In this type of hunting, being out at daybreak has no particular advantage; in fact, there are some positive disadvantages in stationing standers. Each race usually involves six to eight dogs with a driver for every pair of dogs. The drivers help move them in the right general direction, toward the line of standees, and the drivers themselves make as much noise as possible to help the dogs stir things up. If the ratio is much less than one driver per two dogs, it's often hard to round up the pack after a race is over. The favored ploy is to set standers up in either a big horseshoe-shaped arc or a rough S-curve. The drivers then move the dogs into the openings of the S-curve or around the edge of the horseshoe. These two formations offer an opportunity for the maximum number of people to spot game and get shots. Even so, in this jungle of cover, it's very easy for a canny whitetail to slip right by a stander, sometimes passing within 20 or 30 feet.

Many sportsmen hunt together year after year on these drives, espe-

Seen from an unusually good stand in a dog-driving area, a deer crosses in high gear but in the open, where there's no problem identifying a legal target and getting off a good shot.   (Photo: Tom Brakefield)

cially if they belong to one of the hunting clubs which are so prevalent in the South.   The layouts of certain drives become "classics" because they produce, and are used every year.   The stands become well known and, in fact, may be numbered.   To ensure fairness in assigning stands, numbered tags are often drawn by the hunters from a hat and this chance assignment determines which stands they'll occupy.   Then no one can gripe about favoritism, nor do hunters get into any arguments about who is going to hunt where because they want to occupy the same stand.

Most dog hunts are run by a "huntmaster" who is in absolute

charge. If a club is involved, this person is generally elected for a period of a year and serves as an officer of the club. He decides which areas will be hunted when, which dogs and how many will be used, and who the drivers will be. He is responsible for the drawing of the stand numbers and for the positioning of the standers. He also resolves any disputes that may come up about the hunt or the game. In a word, he's boss, and all agree that his word is (for that day or that season, anyway) the final one. After seeing a number of arguments that sometimes occur in Eastern or Midwestern deer camps, some so silly that even the people involved feel pretty sheepish a few hours later, I think this approach might be more widely applied. The huntmaster also sets any fines or other penalties that may be called for by infractions of the rules during a hunt.

This kind of country and this kind of hunting call for buckshot. Although high-powered rifles and slugs are legal in these areas and are often used in the northern portions of the same states, the thick cover and the nature of the hunt demand use of buckshot here. A rifle would be dangerous to the drivers and the other standers, and there's no possibility of long shots, anyway. The 12-gauge gun is far and away the favorite for this type of hunting though the 16 does still have a limited number of advocates. Very few 20's are used in this type of hunting except for youngsters or some novice women hunters. The autoloader and the pump-action both have their advocates, with the autoloader getting the nod about two times out of three. Very few doubles, of either side-by-side or over-and-under persuasion, turn up for this type of gunning.

Three sizes of buckshot are in common use and all have their advocates. The 00 ("Double Ought") size is the largest at .33 caliber with 12 to the standard 2¾-inch 12-gauge shell. The 0, or "Single Ought," runs .32 caliber for each ball and the "No. 1 Buck" is smallest at .30 caliber and 16 to the 12-gauge shell. No. 1 Buck is probably the most popular because of the feeling that the three or four additional pellets increase your chances in heavy cover.

Buckshot can be surprisingly destructive at the near ranges. The first deer I ever took was killed cleanly and quickly with a single pellet at about 40 yards. The deer was threading its way through a thick clump of brush, but, as is so often the case here, I had to settle for that shot or none. However, buckshot should be limited to 75-yard shots—and preferably to 50- to 60-yard ranges, if possible.

It's a good idea for standers never to be stationed closer than 100 yards from each other, farther apart if possible. However, I must admit that often this informal rule is honored more in the breach than the execution. Sometimes there are too many hunters for the number of ideally located stands on a good drive. Then the hunters may be placed within 75 or even 50 yards of each other. This is not quite so dangerous as it may sound.   All details of these hunts, including the location of the stands, are generally plotted on a topographical map, and all hunters walk in together, each dropping off at his prescribed stand.   Thus, each hunter knows exactly where the other hunters are.   And one of the ironclad rules in this type of hunting is: *No stander moves from his stand until the race is officially declared over.*   To break this rule is generally to draw a severe penalty and much criticism.   In this thick cover, it doesn't pay to go waltzing through a bunch of hunters unless you're dressed in orange and singing "America the Beautiful" at the top of your lungs!

It's important for the stander to remain absolutely still and quiet during the race.   Many standers find a comfortable seat for the long and often cramped wait.   This lowers a hunter's silhouette and further reduces any danger of being hit.   Though I grew up in this country and killed my first

A hunt with dogs can be very productive, as shown by this photo of one club's morning harvest.   In hot Southern weather, it's advisable to skin a deer as soon as possible, and that's what the men are doing.   (Photo: Tom Brakefield)

In parts of Canada, dogs serve a far different purpose from their function on Southern club hunts. Instead of driving the deer, they're held in reserve to trail any wounded game that isn't immediately found—a service they also perform in parts of Europe. Well-controlled dogs, used to trail injured game where such a practice is legal, can significantly reduce the number of wounded but lost deer. These five hunters at French River, Ontario, have collected a deer apiece with the aid of their trailing dogs. (Photo: Ontario Dept. of Tourism & Information)

deer here, I have no personal knowledge of any deer-hunting accidents occurring. In this sport as in any other, there must have been accidents over a period of many decades, but most of the hunting has become so ritualized and is so safety-conscious that a remarkable safety record has been established.

Though I would not like to limit my deer hunting solely to this method (just as I wouldn't like to limit it completely to *any* single method), the technique does offer its own particular satisfactions. The unmoving and attentive stand hunter can often see interesting and unusual wildlife sights. I have had squirrels crawl over my boot while waiting, and once I saw a rare sight, a gray fox skulking by some 40 yards away. I was too interested in him and what he was doing to shoot at him.

The sound of the dogs keeps you asking yourself if they're moving your way, and that tends to keep the adrenalin flowing. Also, even if the dogs aren't moving your way with the particular deer they're coursing at the moment, the very fact that they're out there stirring things up always means that you have a chance of seeing a savvy old whitetail buck go skulking by.

There are few or no professional guides or hunting operators in this part of the country. If you'd like to set up a hunt of this type, I suggest writing to the fish and game commission of the state you're interested in and ask for a list of hunting clubs or other possible contacts to help you make arrangements. Sometimes you can even set up a simple hunt with a game warden or field biologist attached to the department if you're an agreeable chap with a sincere interest in learning more about this sport and this part of the country. Hunters here, like hunters the world over, know no barriers of age, social station, or economic status. A good sport and camp companion is always welcome and often it may be possible to trade hunts with someone: You hunt as his guest one year and he visits you the next year. An added bonus is that the deer season in this area often stretches on into January, so a hunter from another region doesn't have to pass up his own local season in order to feel his nerves tingle when he hears the dogs and asks himself, "Are they heading this way?"

6

The Problems of
a Handgun Hunter

by Steve Ferber

Missing a shot—or worse, wounding a deer with a handgun and not recovering the animal—is the most sobering situation the handgun hunter can experience. In the unhappy instant following the gun's report and the observation of the bullet's effect, he stands there wishing, perhaps, that the shot had been attempted with a rifle. The higher risk of missing or only wounding big game by hunting with a handgun rather than a long gun is the chief argument against the sport and is not far removed from some public opinion regarding the hunting of deer with bow and arrow, as well. The argument is valid. It's just plain harder to bring down a deer with a pistol than with a rifle. We all know that.

But not harder because bullets fired from handguns aren't potent medicine. They are. An improperly placed bullet—fired from any gun—won't stop your buck, and one placed properly will. You have to accept your own limitations with a handgun, and adhere to them, in the same way you would with your rifle. These built-in limitations involve the attitude of the target and distance of the target from the shooter. You might attempt a shot on a running buck from 200 yards with a rifle under certain reasonable circumstances, but you and I wouldn't try that same shot with a pistol any more than we would with an arrow. We might, however, try a running shot with a handgun at lesser yardage and favorable conditions.

These conditions can be considered quickly, at the time the target presents itself, by keeping in mind a word common in golf parlance—*par*. Being able to shoot "par" in golf is quite an accomplishment, and is not the rule. But the application of position, attitude, and range in handgun shooting, and the careful weighing of those factors before the decision to shoot is made, should be the rule.

Let's consider *position* first. Our best competition shooters spend hours a day, almost every day, practicing. They practice sight alignment and trigger squeeze, and it's not uncommon for the serious target shooter

A Montana hunter rests his arms over the hood of his 4WD as he lines up his .357 Magnum on a mule deer. If you haven't spotted the target in this photo, follow the line of sight from the gun barrel to the base of the tree a little to the shooter's right. The deer is standing in the open, just below the tree.

to burn up several hundred rounds of ammo during each session.   All their shooting is done from a standing position, using one hand to hold the gun at arm's length, while keeping, usually, both eyes open.   The maximum range is 50 meters (international) or 50 yards (conventional).   A good many of them can hit a target from that distance the size of a pack of cigarettes four out of five times.   It takes enormous effort and expertise to shoot that well under those controlled conditions.   You, as a handgun hunter, don't have to train that way or that hard to become just as good a shot in the field.   In fact, one-handed, unsupported shooting would work against you.   The answer is the two-handed, supported hold.   Lean the gun up against something!

In the field, it's easy.   If you're shooting from a tree stand, for instance, you have branches at your disposal—or even the trunk.   On the ground there might be tree trunks, blowdowns, fenceposts, dirt piles, or whatever; any one of these can become a perfect handgun rest in seconds.

Two things separate handgun champions from second-place winners: consistently good sight alignment and a steady hold.   And without a steady hold, good sight alignment is difficult to achieve.   Again, you don't have to worry as much about a "steady" hold in the field; under most conditions, it's automatic when the gun is resting on a support.   In fact, when the gun is supported that way, your hold will be as solid as mine or anyone else's who might experience the same set of conditions.   Absolute zero movement is not only attainable, it's the rule.   The thing that takes practice is good sight alignment, and there just isn't room for error.   If the front blade is out of alignment with the rear sight by only a small fraction of an inch, the point of impact downrange moves drastically.   Because handguns have such a short sight radius (the distance between the front and rear sights) compared to a typical hunting rifle, sighting errors are extremely common.

Without the benefit of a solid support, such as a tree trunk, and if the terrain won't let you lie prone for your shot, the sitting position is best.   Draw up your knees and lean slightly forward, placing your arms at a point just forward of the elbows on the knees, and place the palm of your non-shooting hand under your shooting hand.   Experiment a little with this position until you're comfortable; experiment further until you've achieved a very steady hold.   It is not difficult.

Your handgun should have adjustable sights—the rear one, that is—for elevation and windage.   Adjust it until you're hitting center when you're aiming center, and during your practice sessions use ear protectors.   Enough other factors contribute to flinching and jerking, so you'd do well by at least eliminating muzzle blast and report.   In your actual hunting situation it won't matter because you'll only be making one shot, or just a few.

Sight-in your gun for 50 yards, and know, too, where the point of impact is at 25, 75, and 100 yards. In my judgment, unless you're really a fine marksman, no deer shot should be attempted with a handgun beyond 75 yards, regardless of what caliber you're using. But virtually any average hunter, who knows his gun and loads and who practiced beforehand, can make consistent kills from distances under 75 yards under the right conditions.

The front blade of your handgun must be aligned perfectly in the center of the rear notch when you make your shot. And you squeeze a handgun trigger, you don't "pull" it as you do with a shotgun. A little practice will show you how to squeeze without disrupting your sight alignment.

Target shooters concentrate on their front sight. That is, their focus is made there, not on the target, not on the rear sight. Rear sight and target are a blur, but by focusing in this way perfect sight alignment is achieved, as well as a very good sight picture (the relationship of rear sight, front sight, and target). Misalign the front sight by 1/100th of an inch using a Colt .45 ACP, and the point of impact will move 3 inches at 50 yards. But achieve perfect sight alignment, and move the gun (which changes the sight picture) a full inch, and the point of impact will only move an inch. The gun shoots where it's aimed. If sight alignment is incorrect, you don't know where it will shoot.

But competitive shooters know their target is not only stationary, they also know their aiming point, the bull, always measures the same. Hunters have a completely different situation, depending on which way the deer is facing, whether he's level with the ground or pointing up- or downhill, or if he's stationary, walking, or running. So first you get your sight picture. Focus on the game, through the sights, and when you're satisfied with the target—neck, heart, or chest—slip your focus back to your front sight to achieve perfect alignment and squeeze off the shot.

The only way to prepare yourself for a hunting situation with a handgun is by practicing at the range. And I don't mean by shooting tin cans— very little is learned about you and your gun that way.

Set up real bull's-eye-type targets at 25, 50, and 75 yards, and another at 100. Sit at the bench or portable table, or on the ground as described earlier, and squeeze off your shots two-handed, first at 25 yards. Adjust your rear sight for windage when you begin to shoot good groups consistently. Then shoot at the 50-yard target, and the 75-yard target. Know the trajectory of the load you're using at these various yardages and adjust your rear sight's vertical setting so you're hitting center-bull at 75 yards. Know where it's hitting at 50 and 25 yards after the sights are set for 75. Then take some shots at the 100-yard target. Know how much the bullet drops so you'll know where to aim should you fail to clean-kill your buck with the first shot at 60 yards—and he wheels and runs.

Practice standing, using a two-handed hold. Face the target dead-on, extend both arms completely, lean back slightly and squeeze off the shot. Compared to sitting and using the knees as a rest, or leaning the gun up against a fencepost, an unsupported two-handed hold is difficult. If you're not in a good position when the deer presents itself, and can't get into a steady position soon enough, don't shoot. But you'll probably be able to hit a chest-size target from 25 yards that way in short order.

Now let's consider the target's *attitude*. If you see a flash of white tail zooming out in front of you, or a deer running through chokecherry vines with all four feet to the wind, or any other "snap-shot" situation, don't try to make the shot. That sort of thing is hard enough with a rifle or shotgun and is usually out of the question with a pistol—particularly in the East where there's generally a lot of thick cover.

But if the attitude of the animal suits you—if the deer doesn't know you're around and is just walking or browsing or standing—get into position and think about taking him. Always try for a chest shot between 50 and 75 yards. Consider a shoulder shot between 25 and 50, and if you're good enough to neck-shoot at 25 yards or under, do it. The important thing, after the shot, is to cock the hammer immediately for a possible second shot. It's far easier and faster, incidentally, to prepare for a second shot with a revolver than with a bolt-action rifle—you only need to move one thumb.

Target attitude is extremely important. You must have perfect sight alignment to make a handgun shot true. It can be done easily if you have time to set up for the shot. You'll miss, or worse, if you haven't the time to do it properly.

What about running shots? In many Western situations, particularly on the slow, inquisitive mule deer, certain moving-target shots are reasonable. Remember this. From a very solid sitting position, as many as six good handgun shots can be made in as little as 15 or 20 seconds. If you are so positioned when a muley begins hopping down—or up—a mountain slope, and you know it will take him at least 30 seconds to reach cover, and he's only 60 or 70 yards away from you to begin with, and you know the lead necessary to make a good shot isn't much, and you *had become a good shot before the hunt began*—you'll take him.

You've noticed that I keep stressing yet another factor: short range. The .357, .41, and .44 Magnum and the Long Colt .45 handgun trajectories are not flat. Some guns, like the Thompson/Center single-shot in .30 Herrett caliber do shoot fairly flat but, as a rule, range is an extremely critical factor in handgun shooting. And don't think you're getting extra "range" by using a .44 Magnum instead of a .357 Magnum. What you're getting is more *punch*. A good shot made from either

It's just about impossible to pick the deer out of the trees, but he's there. In handgun hunting, a solid shooting rest should be used whenever possible, and it's especially important for long shots such as this. There's nothing unsporting about using a hunting vehicle as a rest where it's legal.

caliber will down any deer, and if you can't shoot the heavier-recoiling Magnums as well as you do the .357, for instance, don't take one along.

A 75-yard shot from a handgun is a long shot, as you'll see when you practice at the range. But if you have the time to think out the shot, you can get good sight alignment and make the shot an accurate one. Beyond the range, critical sight alignment is much harder and just shouldn't be attempted by the handgunning sportsman of average skill. Fairly exact range is easier to calculate in the East than in the West. The more open the area, the closer things look; it's that simple. But when fences, orchards, trees, and other objects dot an area between the gun muzzle and the target, 50 or 150 yards is easier to judge accurately.

Case in point. Not too long ago I was on a mule-deer hunt at the Apache Indian Mescalero reservation in New Mexico, an area incorporating 460,000 acres of prime muley country. My Apache guide took me to a place called Morgan Canyon, at an elevation of about

7,500 feet. We began walking the rim of the canyon, and later, when we dropped down into it, we spotted a three-year-old buck and a spike browsing on the edge of a hill about 300 yards away.

The wind was directly in our faces. The guide sat down, drawing his binocular from its case, and sat there watching the action while I began my stalk. Ten minutes later, both bucks were still there; they hadn't been alarmed and were now, I estimated, just 80 yards from me. Deciding not to push my luck, I sat down and got into a solid two-handed knee hold. I was shooting a 6-inch-barreled .357 Magnum Colt Python, with iron sights, and loaded with the 146-grain Speer hollow-point jacketed bullet in front of 18 grains of Winchester 296 Ball powder—a hot, very effective load. (Incidentally, Magnum primers are a must with that first-rate powder.)

I squeezed off a perfect shot, holding on the right shoulder of the bigger buck. It was a quartering shot. The bullet struck several inches low, throwing bark from a blowdown immediately in front of my target. But I *knew* I had made a perfect shot so when he wheeled and began to run I simply aimed higher for the second shot and dropped him.

We paced off the distance and I was surprised to learn that my original range estimate had been short by a full 75 yards, which caused the first shot to hit low. The buck didn't look that far away at the time. He had been standing on a rise on the other side of an arroyo, and I had stalked him for over 100 yards. He just looked closer than he actually was. My guide was likewise surprised when we paced off 147 long steps to the blowdown. It turned out to be the longest deer shot I had ever made—or ever attempted. The bullet passed through the left rump and quartered clear through the rib cage and stopped, perfectly mushroomed, under the skin. With a handgun, then, knowing the animal's range can be as critical as good sight alignment.

What about scope sights on a handgun? They're fine, I think, for varmint shooting, and also for most Western deer-hunting situations—where the country is often open. It takes considerably longer to find your target in a telescope than through open sights, and if additional shots are needed, and the deer's cover is nearby, there's a fair chance you'll never pick him up in your scope before he disappears. Of course, aside from the advantage of seeing better with a scope, the other obvious advantage of using one is the fact that you needn't worry about sight alignment. If you've sighted-in your handgun properly, the bullet will hit at the point where your crosshairs are positioned on the game animal. But with iron sights, you're ready to shoot faster.

One of my favorite handgun cartridges for deer is the .357 Magnum, properly loaded. The .41 Magnum and .44 Magnum are also sensational cartridges. The .44 gives a big wallop to the shooter, so the caliber requires additional practice to use effectively in hunting situations. If you shoot a .270 rifle regularly, for instance, and then pick up a .300 Weatherby Magnum, you'll notice that the additional recoil and muzzle blast of the heavier gun will work against you, reducing your accuracy until you learn to handle it. And some people are recoil-shy enough so that they never learn to shoot the heavier-hitting guns well. This is true of handgun shooters as well as riflemen. You should hunt deer with the gun and caliber you shoot best. Chest-shoot a deer with any of the calibers I've mentioned and you've collected your trophy.

The .45 Long Colt, properly loaded, is also a fine deer cartridge. A friend of mine loads 11 grains of Unique behind Speer's 225-grain bullet in that caliber, shoots it in the Colt Frontier Model revolver, and gets about 1,150 feet per second—a proof load plus. A safer load (in a modern gun) would be 9 grains of the same powder, working up, possibly, to 10 grains. Though we're talking about the very old .45 Long Colt cartridge, those particular loads are definitely Magnum-types.

Unique powder has been a first-rate pistol powder for generations, the choice of many Magnum handgun shooters. But two problems with it have always been incomplete burning and lack of bulk in most cartridge cases. One of the best, newest, Magnum pistol powders I've found to date is Winchester 296, a Ball powder that not only burns extremely well in Magnum loads but also fills the cartridge case, either eliminating air space entirely or guaranteeing a minimum of air space between powder and bullet. As I said earlier, this Ball powder requires Magnum primers for good ignition. Having mentioned powders for handloading, I should add that plenty of good bullets are available from a number of manufacturers. For deer hunting, my own recommendation is to use a bullet weight of at least 140 grains in the calibers I've been discussing. For .44 Magnum deer loads, a variety of good .429-diameter bullets are available in weights from 200 to 240 grains.

Which gun to use? For most deer-hunting situations, a revolver is best because of safety, and ease of handling, as well as accuracy. Don't hunt deer with a Magnum having a barrel length of less than 6 inches. A 6-inch, or longer, barrel allows for a good sight radius. Even more important, shorter-barreled guns will not offer optimum velocity of the bullet or complete burning of the powder.

Revolvers by Ruger, Smith & Wesson, Colt, and Dan Wesson—and a few other manufacturers—are first-rate from the standpoint of both strength and accuracy. The single-shot Thompson/Center gun is also a strong and accurate product, the .30-caliber Herrett cartridge (shortened and necked-down .30/30 case) being the latest addition to T/C's list of calibers. Properly loaded, it's an enormously accurate and powerful load, and even though the bullets for the cartridge weigh 110 to 130 grains,

Coming down from a high Montana slope, two hunting partners drag out a fine buck mule deer. Even with the buck dressed out and only a few more yards to go to the pickup, this is heavy work. The lightness and compactness of a handgun (in this case a Ruger .44 Magnum) are among its hunting attractions. (Photo: Montana Chamber of Commerce)

it's an effective deer cartridge because of the average velocity (2,000 to 2,400-plus fps).

You can certainly hand-pick conditions where a single-shot like the Thompson/Center will be more than fine, or even a big semi-auto like the Harry Sanford-designed Auto-Mag Pistol—an almost all stainless-steel gun that shoots the .357 AMP and .44 AMP cartridges, which are both Magnums, and the only semi-auto Magnums in existence.

But for general deer hunting, when you're not sure of the kind of shot you'll be offered, a revolver is, in my judgment, your best bet.

7

Black-Powder Bonanza

by B. R. Hughes

Dawn came slowly to the heavily forested ridge bordering La Pile Creek in southeastern Arkansas that misty, cold December morning. The hunter sat with his back against a large pine tree, watching a game trail at the base of the ridge. Despite his blaze-orange down jacket, warm pants, and insulated boots, there was no denying that he was cold.

A flight of mallards, apparently heading for nearby Open Brake, caught the hunter's eye, and when he lowered his gaze to the path, there, perhaps 65 yards away, where nothing had been visible a few seconds previously, stood a six-point whitetail buck, cautiously slipping along.

Carefully, slowly, the sportsman raised his rifle, centered the blade of his front sight in the V of the rear on the shoulder of the buck and gently—ever so gently—squeezed the trigger. At the report, the deer broke into a stumbling run and disappeared down the trail. The hunter approached the spot where the deer had been standing at the time of the shot, and noted with satisfaction a spray of blood. No more than 50 yards away he found the body of the buck. The slug had hit the deer through the lungs, and all that remained was to field-dress the whitetail and get it to his pickup truck, some 300 yards away.

This scene, or one very similar to it, took place numerous times in many different locales last season. There was one factor, however, that makes this particular hunter the exception to the rank and file: his rifle was a muzzleloader.

According to figures released by the National Shooting Sports Foundation, muzzleloading is one of the fastest-growing of the many shooting activities. While it's difficult to put an exact total on the number of men and women who enjoy using such guns, those in the know say that there are more than 200,000 individuals who shoot black-powder guns on a more or less regular basis, and the number is growing steadily.

Why should a person use such a gun? A difficult question to answer, but part of it is probably related to a desire to return to a simpler era. Many seek some release from their everyday worries, and if a person receives enjoyment from shooting front-loaders like those in daily use perhaps 150 years ago, it's a harmless and wholesome pastime. Then there are those who maintain that using a high-powered rifle with a telescopic sight makes taking game too easy. Most such sportsmen are veteran outdoorsmen looking for a new challenge. It is my contention that a muzzleloader is a much more sporting arm than a bow, but that is another story.

Those who imagine that the modern deer hunter who uses a front-loader is working under a tremendous handicap are in for a tremendous surprise when they test their first good muzzleloader. I have always felt that the average quality percussion rifle with open sights is about as accurate out to approximately 100 yards as the typical modern lever-action .30/30. Moreover, good cap-and-ball rifles are extremely reliable, provided they're given some care and consideration.

If a man has in mind collecting deer-size game with a muzzleloader, then I suggest that absolutely nothing smaller than a .50-caliber be selected, and this should be considered barely adequate for such game. This is not to say that thousands of deer have not been collected with .36s and .45s, but the same could be said of the .22 Long Rifle. When it comes to optimum calibers, either the .54 or .58 will prove a much more reliable arm than any smaller bore.

Mark it well: A heavily loaded .54 or .58 will provide more punch at modest ranges than will the .45/70 factory load. Thus, the man who states that black powder should not be used for big game simply does not understand the potential of a full load of FFG black powder in a large-bore front-loader. It has been my experience that a good .54-caliber rifle, for example, loaded with a patched .535 round ball weighing approximately 220 grains, and backed with 110 grains of FFG powder, will develop more "knock-down" effect out to about 75 yards than will, for example, a 200-grain slug from the .35 Remington cartridge. The paper ballistics show more than 1,400 foot-pounds of energy at the muzzle, and this is not truly indicative of its actual power.

When round balls are used for hunting, some consideration must be given to the patch lubricant. While many shooters use saliva for match shooting, this is not at all a sage idea for hunting, because the rifle will be loaded in the morning and perhaps not fired until late in the afternoon, if indeed at all. It doesn't take long for the saliva to dry out, and you are then in reality shooting an unlubed patch, and while such a load may shoot well enough, this is almost a sure-fire way to rust and ruin your chamber. There are a number of excellent commercial lubricants on the market, and, for what it's worth, my favorite is Thompson/Center's Maxi-Lube. Many shooters swear by Crisco or Vaseline, and as long as you're

The 100-yard group was punched in this target by the Allen & Thurber replica propped against the stump. This group shows that a .50-caliber muzzleloader is sufficiently accurate for shots at deer within moderate range.

shooting in relatively warm weather, these two substances certainly do a very good job.

Many experienced shooters feel that a front-loader is much more effective when used on medium to large game if a Minie ball is used instead of a round, patched ball. A Minie is nothing more than a hollow-based conical slug which loads easily and expands to fill the bore when the powder ignites. I will readily concede that were I to go deer hunting with a front-loading rifle with a bore smaller than .50-caliber, I would certainly use a Minie. A typical .45-caliber Minie ball will weigh 265 grains, and 60 grains of FFFG black powder will drive the slug at approximately 1,425 fps at the muzzle. This translates out to about 1,200 foot-pounds of energy. Otherwise, I prefer a patched round ball for deer, primarily because I have generally obtained somewhat superior accuracy with this projectile.

Occasionally I read where some misguided soul has suggested loading

Half-stocked Plains rifles of this sort are among the most popular black-powder arms for deer hunting, and the author recommends them. As to bore size, Hughes feels that nothing smaller than .50 caliber should be used by a muzzleloading deer hunter.

two patched balls atop a normal powder load in an effort to improve the potency of a muzzleloader. In my opinion this is a dangerous practice and one that I cannot recommend under any circumstance. When the old-timers needed more power, they went to a bigger bore. This is still a good rule. If your .45- or .50-caliber rifle isn't adequate for the task, go to either a .54 or a .58.

Were I choosing a muzzleloading rifle strictly for deer and larger game, there is no question in my mind but that the .54 is the ideal caliber. This was a favorite bore size of the Mountain Men, and their predilection for this caliber was no idle whim.

The man looking for his first front-loading rifle is very likely to purchase a gun that looks flashy and costs perhaps $100 less than some of the "name" brands on today's market. Generally this is a mistake. There are a number of half-stock Plains rifles on the market at this time that list from perhaps $150 to $250. Within these limits it is possible to purchase a front-loader that will prove accurate, safe, and long-lived. I have a decided preference for the percussion rifle, and I think that any beginner who purchases a flintlock is soon going to regret his selection. First-class muzzleloading marksmen can shoot flinters about as well as percussion rifles, but there aren't many first-class marksmen of any type around today, much less front-loaders. Moreover, to obtain comparable value in a flintlock, you should be prepared to spend considerably more than you would for a percussion model.

The traditional Long Rifle has received no space at all to this point in my discussion simply because I do not feel that there is a Kentucky, as these rifles are popularly called, currently available in a factory model that represents solid dollar value. The best buys I've seen to date for the man who wants a Long Rifle are those offered by Don Lamotte, Route 1, Box

Before the hunt, a muzzleloading rifle should be checked out with the load that will be used for deer. If no bench is handy, sandbags on an automobile top will serve quite well as a rest.

25C, Newland, North Carolina 28657.   Don gets around $300 for a standard rifle, and there is a considerable waiting period, but they are beautifully made and shoot exceedingly well.   They are not, however, ordinarily available in calibers larger than .45.

The better-made Civil War replicas are good values, and it is possible to purchase such a gun for well under $200.   These rifles, which generally come in .58-caliber, make dandy hunting arms.   Tops in this class is the 1861 Enfield replica imported by Jana, Inc.   This model retails at about $225, and it is a whale of a buy.

With no hesitancy at all, I can safely say that the number-one buy currently available for the man interested in a front-loading hunting rifle is Thompson/Center's .54 Renegade, which is a well-made, accurate rifle, and, perhaps best of all, it costs only about $165.

It is certainly not necessary to spend $400 or so for a decent muzzleloader.   As a matter of fact, a few of the $400 rifles that I have examined in recent months show signs of sloppy workmanship.   This is not to say that there are no expensive muzzleloaders worth their price; one has only to examine the artistry of a John Bivins, for example, to realize that here is an $800 investment that is sure to increase in value as the years go by.   Unfortunately, however, paying a big price is no guarantee of quality.

Conversely, the series of under-hammer models offered by Numrich Arms represent a top buy.   It is possible to buy one of these models for around $100, and they are perfectly suitable for hunting and possess better than acceptable accuracy.   The Numrich Deer Stalker, a .58, is the "pick of the litter" as far as I am concerned.

Let's suppose you've selected your front-loading rifle.   The first problem that will confront you is deciding upon a load.   For target shooting I prefer charges running around one grain of powder "per caliber."   For example, in a .45 I generally use about 45 grains of powder.   For hunting, however, heavier charges are needed.   (*Note:* Civil War replicas should not be used with charges exceeding approximately 65 grains of powder.)   With the heavier-barreled Plains rifles a good hunting load would be 2 grains of powder per caliber.   In a .54 this would translate out to 108 grains, which makes a dandy load.

When it comes to a selection of powder, the rule of thumb is to use FFFG powder in calibers up to and including .50, and FFG powder in calibers larger than .50.   This works very well in practice, and there is no good reason not to follow this simple guide.

Should you follow my lead and stick pretty much to the patched round ball for hunting, you should give some attention to the selection of a good patch material.   Unfortunately, old tee shirts, bath towels, etc., do not lend themselves to this use.   Pillow ticking is good, as is blue denim, only

Hunter Raymond Rhodes kneels for a picture with a fine Texas whitetail buck and the rifle that took it. The gun is a .58 Texas Carbine, and Rhodes used a Minie ball in the muzzleloader to collect this trophy. (Photo: Hal Swiggett)

be sure to wash your material several times to get rid of the sizing before using it. A properly lubed patched ball should require some effort to push it down the barrel, but not extreme force. It should go down with one firm sustained push. Ideally, the barrel should be swabbed after every shot. If this practice is not followed, the barrel will foul and considerable effort will be required to seat the ball. Some shooters believe in fouling the barrel before loading for hunting, but if you sight-in your rifle with a clean bore, wiping it after every shot, there is no reason why the barrel should be fouled.   Any oil in the barrel, however, should be wiped out before loading.   The barrel should be clean and dry.

One make of percussion cap is probably as good as another, but you should by all means use the same size and brand for hunting as you used to sight-in your rifle.

When it comes to sights, I have seen practically everything used on a muzzleloader, including telescopic sights, tang sights, peep sights, and open rear types.   Any good sights will bring home the venison.   Many find the use of a scope on a front-loader distasteful, since the Mountain Men didn't use them.   The Mountain Men didn't melt the lead for their bullets over a gas burner or in an electric pot, either.   The biggest disadvantage to the use of a telescopic sight on a front-loader that I have found is that the rear lens will get scratched and smudged from the bits and pieces of percussion cap that fly around everytime such a gun is touched off.   This is not true, however, with the Numrich under-hammer models or the Harrington & Richardson break-action Huntsman.   If your eyes are a bit old or tired, you might well consider the use of a scope with one of these rifles.   After all, you have a greater obligation to the game to place your shot well than you do to tradition.

Personally, I prefer the old-fashioned open rear sight with a blade front.   Since the trajectory of a muzzleloader cannot be considered flat by any standard—except perhaps by comparison with an arrow or a thrown rock—the maximum effective range of the typical front-loader is no more than 125 yards or so.   Which is not to say that game has not and will not be taken cleanly at more extreme yardage with a muzzleloader.   Iron sights do very well at modest range, and the man using a front-loader should make every effort to get as close as possible to his target before pulling the trigger.   I seriously doubt if there is ever any sporting occasion when a shot should be taken at a deer with a muzzleloader at a distance exceeding 150 yards or so.   Remember the .54 round ball we mentioned earlier that was kicking up more than 1,400 foot-pounds of energy at the muzzle?   Well, by the time that ball has reached 100 yards, it is developing only about 540 foot-pounds of energy!   Not an impressive figure by any standard.   If you plan to do some long-range shooting at game animals with your front-loader, then I would suggest the use of a Minie ball instead of a patched round ball.

It's been said before, but it's worth saying again: Never, never shoot anything but black powder in a muzzleloader!   It should also be remembered that a front-loader must be cleaned regularly.   My rule is that if I shoot on a given day, the gun must be cleaned that same day.   The best procedure is to use boiling water, allow the barrel to dry, then swab out the barrel, first with dry patches, then with a lightly oiled patch.   Before loading it again, a dry patch should be run down the barrel.

When hunting I like to place a fresh load in the rifle at the beginning of each day. Snap a couple or three caps on the nipple before loading to make sure there is no oil in this area. How do I unload my gun from the previous day's hunt? Simply by firing it into a clay bank or other safe backstop. Then I clean it before going to bed. The next morning I push a dry patch down the barrel and load it. Won't the explosion of the charge frighten the deer in the area? I seriously doubt it, as the sound of the gun is little different from thunder, which the game hears on a regular basis.

If you cannot stand the thought of discharging a gun in game country unnecessarily, at the close of the day's hunting, uncap your rifle and securely tie a piece of plastic around the end of the muzzle; then place a piece of this plastic material over the nipple and fully lower the hammer on it. Stand the rifle, muzzle end down, propped so that it cannot be knocked over, and the load should function properly the next day. If you stand the rifle muzzle up, there is an excellent chance that grease or oil may foul things up. After the hunt, clean your gun thoroughly, and it should last you a lifetime.

A number of states now have special seasons for muzzleloaders, just as they do for bowhunters. This is something I oppose, and my reasoning is simple: If you feel you are hunting game with an inferior weapon, then in fairness to the game you should instead use something in which you have perfect confidence. An adequate arm is just that, and I feel no handicap in hunting with a muzzleloader during the regular season. After all, there is no special duck season for those of us who hunt with a muzzleloader, nor is there a special squirrel season, quail season, etc. Why should there be a special deer season? There is a special season for deer in a wildlife management area only about an hour's drive from my home. I haven't been there, and I'm not going. If you feel otherwise, have at it! There are special seasons in some areas, and this is still supposed to be a free country.

The man carrying a big-bore quality percussion rifle doesn't have to take a back seat to any nimrod, provided he can get into comfortable range with that front-loader and make his first shot count! If this makes you feel just a bit like Kit Carson, well, that's not a bad bonus, is it?

8

The Pros and Cons of Bowhunting

by Russell Tinsley

Archery is enjoying phenomenal growth. Industry estimates place the upsurge at between 35 and 40 percent for each of the past two years. A substantial share, some 70 percent, of this new business was hunting equipment—or tackle, as some bowmen prefer to call it. But getting equipped doesn't automatically qualify anyone for the title of bowhunter. Some of the newcomers give the sport a brief fling, become discouraged, and quit. As in a marathon race, there are many who start but few who cross the finish line. Determination is the primary key that separates those-that-do from those-that-don't.

Make no mistake, it is a demanding, challenging sport. You *earn* every deer you down with an arrow. In hunting deer with bow and arrow, there are many things that can go wrong—and something usually does! It can be frustrating and exasperating at times. Rewarding, too, even if bowhunting success can't always be measured in terms of filling the freezer. As the famed archer Fred Bear has said, bowhunting emphasizes the pursuit and chase rather than the kill. If bringing home venison were the only criterion, the sport might be called "deer killing" rather than "deer hunting."

I am no purist. Much of my hunting is done with firearms and that, too, is great sport. I like bowhunting not only for the challenge, but also because it extends my hunting time, thanks to special early seasons for bowhunters only.

Because of increased hunting pressure, you might see a future trend toward making a hunter select either the bow season or the regular season but not both, yet in most states as of now, you can participate in the early archery season and, if you fail to get your deer, you can then hunt with a firearm during the regular season. In a few states, if a hunter is skilled (and lucky, perhaps) he can take a deer during the bow season and another one during the firearms season. Laws vary widely from state to state, so you must get a copy of your state's hunting regulations and determine precisely what you can or cannot do.

Deer traffic is the key to picking a stand, and it's even more important in bowhunting than in rifle hunting because the archer's range is so limited. The author is shown examining tracks in a heavily used game trail. Note Tinsley's camouflage clothing and the camouflage wrapping on the bow. He's also using a bow silencer to deaden the twang of the bowstring, because the sound can make a deer bound in the instant before a relatively slow-moving arrow reaches its mark. (Photo: Russell Tinsley)

Some areas where firearms hunting is prohibited are opened to the bowhunter. That's another bonus. Because of the limitations of his weapon, the archer is less of a threat in densely populated areas or near domestic livestock. I've personally found that the bowhunter stands a much better chance of gaining access to private property than does the gun hunter, and more whitetails are taken on private than on public lands.

Do these "pros" offset the "cons"? It depends on the individual. With bowhunting you definitely pay a price for success. The task of killing a deer with an arrow is tough enough to keep the nationwide success ratio somewhere below 10 percent.

Consider what's involved. Your quarry must be close—plenty close. Each archer has his personal limitations and he must recognize them and not take shots based more on hope than skill. To do so only results in crippled game. My own maximum range is 30 yards, and I prefer the deer to be even closer than that, less than 20 yards if possible. The closer your target, the less margin for error.

You must also know your quarry and its behavior. All things considered, a mule deer is less spooky and nervous than its whitetail cousin. This is particularly true of younger deer (an old muley buck is crafty as hell!). The whitetail deer's nervous system is wound tighter than a watchspring. Just getting one within bow-and-arrow range is no guarantee of success, although that, in itself, is a formidable challenge.

There is no weakness in the deer's defense system. You, the hunter, must negate its senses of smell, sight, and hearing. If you are furtive and patiently quiet, you can stalk and shoot a mule deer, but when after the more widespread whitetail, pragmatic judgment almost demands that you try to ambush an unsuspecting deer from a stand, preferably an elevated or tree stand rather than one at ground level. Up like this, the hunter is above the deer's normal line of sight. He can sit quietly to avoid any telltale commotion, and if there are capricious wind currents the human scent will be swirled off the ground rather than along it. Human odor is one danger signal that no deer ignores.

Yet if you are hunting an area where climbing trees is not permitted, (maybe lands owned by a timber company) you'll have to hunt from a ground-level stand and make do. Deer are killed from such stands. It only makes the task a bit more difficult. Why? That's a natural ques-

OPPOSITE PAGE: A fairly recent development, the strange-looking compound bow has already earned great popularity among big-game archers. It provides tremendous power and velocity with a pull that can be mastered by any hunter of average strength. (Photo: Russell Tinsley)

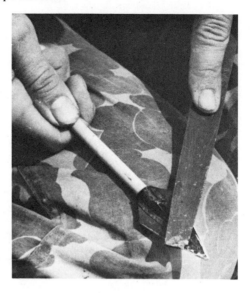

Since an arrow takes game via hemorrhage rather than shock and massive tissue displacement, a razor-sharp broadhead is needed. Every head should be kept sharp enough to shave hair. (Photo: Russell Tinsley)

tion for anyone not familiar with bowhunting.   The range limitation of the weapon has virtually everything to do with it.

When a deer is at close range, the scent factor always is a problem.   It is disconcerting to have a deer come your way and then, if the breeze inexplicably shifts, the critter vanishes much quicker than it appeared on the scene.   To help offset this problem the hunter uses scents, to maybe confuse the deer just long enough so an archer has time to get off an arrow.   There are many commercial scents with pungent odors of such variety as apples and cedar.   My favorite is pure skunk musk.   No, to answer the obvious inquiry, you don't put it on your clothing.   Personally, I simply uncap a bottle of the malodorous liquid and place it slightly downwind from my stand.   The familiar skunk smell is one of the few scents I know that will overpower human odor.   The only source I'm familiar with that handles skunk musk is the mail-order house of Burnham Brothers, Marble Falls, Texas 78654.

All right, by paying careful attention to the prevailing breeze and using scents wisely, you're able to watch as a deer comes within range.   Now you must get your bow up, draw and release the arrow—without the deer being aware of your presence.   Otherwise the critter will spook and run or simply sidestep the arrow. That brings us to the sound factor. Accidently brush your bow against an overhanging limb and the almost imperceptible noise will make the deer suspicious. The chances of your connecting with an arrow are suddenly much reduced.

The successful bowhunter pays careful attention to every detail, no matter how insignificant it might seem. He is well camouflaged, even to putting a mesh headnet on or streaking his face with grease paint—anything to diffuse his outline and make it more difficult for a deer to detect his presence. He is constantly aware of wind direction. When he gets on his stand he looks closely for any obstruction that might get in his

Arguments persist as to whether commercial scents have any attraction whatever for a deer, but there's no doubt that they help cover human odor and thus improve the chance of a close shot before a skittish buck is spooked. (Photo: Russell Tinsley)

way as he brings his bow into shooting position. He has adequate equipment and has become proficient in its use. His broadhead is honed to razor sharpness, for he realizes that an arrow kills by hemorrhage rather than shock and he wants cutting edges which will result in massive bleeding. He knows to aim at a specific spot rather'than at a vague general part of the animal, pinpointing his arrow into vital organs.

If everything is just right up to this crucial point, the hunter still may be dismayed to see his arrow miss its mark, perhaps thrown off by a jerky release or because the deer leaps aside a split second before the projectile arrives—''jumping the string,'' as it is called. Sound travels faster than an arrow; thus the deer may hear the twang of the bowstring and react before the arrow arrives. There are attachments to quiet the string, but they are far from perfect. This, then, is another reason for getting a deer close as possible. There is less chance that it can react before the arrow gets there.

All this well-planned strategy is meaningless, of course, unless the bowhunter is in an area inhabited by deer and has positioned his stand so that he has a reasonable chance of one wandering by within bow range. This means being intimately familiar with your hunting territory. Spend much time in the woods, both prior to and during the season to determine where the animals are likely to be found and their travel routes to and from feeding and bedding areas. There is no shortcut to success. Preparation requires dedication and hard work.

Still not discouraged? If so, then perhaps you are a candidate to join the bowhunting ranks, willing to spend the time and effort to learn how to shoot proficiently, then outwit a wily deer under the most demanding ground rules. It won't be easy. Learning to shoot the bow and arrow requires mastering some basic fundamentals and repetitious practice. The more you shoot, the better you get. Shooting a shotgun or rifle is more easily learned. Comparing the two is like throwing a golf ball straight and true down the fairway or trying to hit it that way with a club. Consistency is a combination of acquired skill and practice.

Getting started correctly cannot be stressed enough. Avoid bad habits and you're on the road to eventual success. To begin with, do some research either by buying a book or obtaining one at your local library. A volume I can recommend is *Bow Hunter's Guide* (Stoeger Publications) and let it be known that I agree with everything the author says. I should—I wrote the book!

In it I am pretty emphatic about some things. You must buy quality equipment of the right type. The bow, either the conventional recurve or the newer compound with its pulleys and cables, should have at least a 45-pound pull, even heavier if you can handle it. The more power, the more velocity and penetration you get with an arrow. And as for that

This is the kind of ideal shot—at least theoretically—that can result from a combination of skill, patience, and a dash of luck.   But even now something can go wrong; the slightest noise, for instance, can send the buck bounding before the arrow reaches him.   (Photo: Russell Tinsley)

arrow, buy the best you can afford. Aluminum, with its more precise manufacturing quality, is my first choice, followed by fiberglass. Cheap wood arrows simply do not have the accuracy and durability of these two products. It makes no sense to go to the expense of a deer-hunting trip, practice and plan, only to blow your chance of killing a deer by false economy; that is, save pennies on a cheap arrow that you can't shoot accurately. And the weight of the arrows must be matched to the weight of the bow. Balanced equipment is vital to accuracy and consistency. A fundamentally sound start is a major step in the right direction. Becoming consistently proficient with a weapon as imprecise as the bow is difficult enough without trying to overcome bad habits. Seek advice from a pro or at least an experienced bowhunter.

Take advantage of every available aid, from camouflage to scents and bow silencers. The bowhunter who is adequately prepared is confident, and confidence sometimes draws that faint line between success and failure.

If you're a gun hunter you must undergo some personal rehabilitation. Admit it or not, a far-shooting, repeating rifle tends to become a subconscious crutch for our limitations. In the open West, for example, mule-deer kills at 300 yards plus are not uncommon. Even if a whitetail buck is spooked from dense undergrowth and the hunter swings on the fleeing animal and misses, he can promptly jack in a fresh round and try again. The bowhunter seldom enjoys the luxury of a second chance. Bowhunting demands the ultimate blend of shooting and hunting skill. Of course, the bow, like the rifle, is merely a tool, nothing more. It is only the means to an end and not the exalted end itself. Nonetheless, there is a certain personal satisfaction to bowhunting that is difficult to describe. You need only to experience it to fully understand what I mean.

Take my case as an example. I've killed numerous deer, both muleys and whitetails. Shooting a run-of-the-mill buck with a rifle no longer holds great excitement for me. But a trophy-size buck—well, that's a different story. That "big one" is what keeps a rifle in my hands during the season. I turned to bowhunting because I was searching for something different, another challenge. It also gave me the opportunity to take advantage of the early special seasons, which in some states are quite liberal. But the bow has made me a bit more humble. With a rifle a buck has to be a pretty impressive specimen before I'll pull the trigger;

OPPOSITE PAGE: Tinsley kneels to examine a fine eight-point whitetail he killed cleanly with a broadhead. (Photo: Russell Tinsley) with a bow I'm not as selective. In fact, you might say I am totally liberated. Let a forkhorn buck or maybe a doe—any shootable and legal deer—blunder within range and the critter better start taking evasive action in a hurry. I can't speak for other bowhunters, but for me every deer I bring home is a trophy. Yes, even a doe at times.

When armed with bow and arrows, just watching a doe meandering down a trail, drawing closer and closer, speeds my heartbeat. Perhaps it is the slow-motion way the drama unfolds, adding to the suspense and anticipation. Or maybe I'm watching around a stand, and I turn my attention in one direction, then when I glance back, there stands a deer, almost as if it had appeared by magic. The critter is close, real close. A very dramatic happening.

A couple of seasons back I was sitting in a low fork of an oak tree among a cluster of oaks that had produced a bumper crop of acorns. The landowner told me he'd seen an eight-point buck coming to this spot almost every late afternoon to feed. He suggested which tree I should climb into and wait.

"He'll be along," the rancher assured me. "Just be patient."

Soon after I had gotten settled comfortably, two deer, a spike buck and a doe, arrived on the scene and they ambled nearby, nibbling at fallen acorns. It wasn't long before another spike buck showed up, almost a twin to the first. The gathering was beginning to look like a family reunion.

I sat absolutely motionless, almost afraid to breathe, determined not to slap at the buzzing mosquitos tormenting my face, fearing that the slightest distraction would frighten the deer and their alarm perhaps would spook the eight-pointer if he was somewhere in the vicinity. One spike was feeding almost directly beneath me, not 10 feet away. Normally a buck that close would be flirting with disaster. But I was confident the bigger buck eventually would be mine. *Patience,* I cautioned myself.

As I waited and hoped, I recalled something that had happened the prior season and I wondered, with some trepidation, if history would repeat itself.

Jerry Wenmohs and I were hidden in a blind he had built near some oaks. The ground blind was well arranged, with ample room inside to maneuver, and openings through which to get off a shot no matter from which direction a deer might approach. Here on his father's ranch, Jerry had told me, he'd seen several bucks visiting the area to forage on acorns.

It wasn't long before one did, indeed, arrive and it was a handsome eight-pointer that any bowman would have been proud to claim. The buck paused at an oak tree maybe 60 yards from our stand. He picked up what acorns had dropped, then lifted his head, stuck his antlers among the low-hanging branches, and shook his head vigorously, knocking more mast to the ground.

Jerry wanted me to take a crack at him, but I said the range was too far, too much of a gamble. The buck probably would wander closer and I would get a much better opportunity.

The whitetail deer is totally unpredictable and things seldom work out exactly as you plan. This buck fed just briefly, ten minutes or less at the same tree, then turned and nonchalantly walked away, in the opposite direction. Just like that, he was gone. Very frustrating, but I didn't regret not taking the shot. At that range—for me, anyway—too many things could go wrong.

Well, back to live action. As things turned out on this shirtsleeves October afternoon, the anticipated eight-point buck never showed. What happened, I don't know. Maybe he had a suspicion that danger lurked in the oak grove. The two spike bucks eventually got their fill and wandered away. By nightfall my nerves were shot. Yet it had been a fascinating experience, merely sitting and watching the deer. When a person observes the nervous animals this way, up close, it is amazing how much he learns.

So the bow, with its obvious limitations, has made me a better hunter. I've trained myself to be more observant of signs such as tracks, scrapes, and droppings. It is a matter of selective focus rather than taking in the whole picture. You begin to see things you've overlooked or ignored before. As for me, even if I fail to get a deer during the early season, the actual hunting is time well spent, for I am scouting areas I later will hunt with my rifle.

Bowhunting to me has been sort of a graduate course in deer behavior. I have killed less but enjoyed it more. I have been fortunate to collect a few deer with arrows, and each adventure is permanently imprinted in my memory. That's the way it is when you accept the challenge of the bow and arrow.

PART II

America's Whitetails

9

The Woodlots of the East

by L. James Bashline

From Maine to Georgia, the Appalachian Mountains are considered "Eastern" deer country. The adjacent geography that extends to the east and west of this range for 200 miles in some cases is different in character, but for hunting purposes it is still the same general type of real estate. Combination stands of conifers and hardwoods are the typical Eastern deer woods and this flora is the main reason whitetails are so abundant there. Before man and his need for lumber reduced the nearly solid stands of huge pine and hemlock timber to a mere shadow of what they once were, whitetail deer were not nearly so plentiful in the East.

The towering pines prevented much undergrowth from taking root and deer food was extremely scarce. By 1910, practically all of the native pine and hemlock were gone. Vast areas were left in an almost barren condition. Surprisingly, little pine regenerated. Instead, dormant seeds of hardwood species and woody shrubs began to cover the Eastern hills and with a bit of help from artificial stocking and enlightened legislation, the whitetail deer began to fill the void. The black cherry, maple, ash, sassafras, black birch, and other succulent shoots were exactly to the deer's liking, and the rest is history.

An annual harvest of 100,000 deer is considered standard for Pennsylvania these days. New York State's harvest is usually just a few thousand under that, and even small states like New Jersey, Maine, Vermont, and New Hampshire post 20,000 or more each year. Indeed, the whitetail deer is in no danger of being eliminated in the East. The problem is keeping the population in check rather than increasing the output of venison.

With all these deer available, it would seem that hunting them must be a snap. Yet the success ratio of Eastern hunters is not close to that enjoyed by Westerners. Admittedly, the hunting pressure is greater in the East and there are probably more hunters afield, say, in Pennsylvania than in any five Rocky Mountain states put together on any deer-hunting day. But does that fully explain the rather poor ratio of one deer for about every eight hunters who hit the woods? The ratio most hunters are concerned with is their own ratio. How many seasons do they connect? The other guy can take care of himself. How can I attain a better batting average?

All successful hunters I have known are quick to point out that they never underestimate the craftiness of the whitetail deer. Many well-traveled big-game chasers who have sampled the best the world has to offer consider the whitetail the most elusive of trophies. Not just an ordinary deer with antlers mind you, but an honest-to-goodness trophy buck. Anyone who has hunted deer for more than a few seasons knows that putting your tag on a less than magnificent spike buck or even a baldy can be full of frustration. Magnify that times ten and you have some idea of how hard it is to come up with a whitetail that would make a respectable wall-hanger.

Eastern whitetails are smart. They have to be. Living in proximity to man has made them that way. Conversely, in deep-woods habitat, deer that seldom see a human being spook at the smell of man. A one-on-one situation in Maine's cedar swamps can be the toughest sort of hunt imaginable. Just as difficult is the small woodlot deer that lives in Hunterdon County, New Jersey. That deer sees humans almost every day of his life. He has learned to feed mostly at night and when pursued can make a veritable army of hunters look extremely foolish. He knows all of the byways of his relatively small bailiwick and takes advantage of every available bit of cover.

In most Eastern states with the exception of Connecticut, Massachusetts, and New Jersey, there is considerable public land for deer hunters to operate on. Maps, available from the respective conservation agencies in most states, illustrate just where the public land is. In spite of increased pressure from militant protectionists, most large landowners will permit hunters to enter their acreage for deer hunting. They should be asked for permission to hunt, however. Eastern hunters depend heavily on private land and, while I hate to be "preachy," hunters must be more respectful of private land in the future. The right to hunt is not a God-given favor just because a hunting license has been purchased. A good relationship with private landowners must be maintained.

In the small woodlots there are three basic methods of hunting that prove successful. The first is the watch-and-wait method. This is simply the old stump-hunter style that requires you to watch a popular trail or keep a steady eye on known feeding areas, such as an orchard or clearing edge. The basic requirement for the hunter in this case is to stay put and avoid all unnecessary movements and sounds. A stump hunter who coughs, sneezes, crackles potato-chip bags, and otherwise converses with

Cut-over patches amid standing timber—including much second growth—are typical of the deer woods throughout great parts of the Appalachian chain. This picture, taken in Maine, shows the author employing one of the classic Eastern techniques, still-hunting combined with stand-hunting. Many of the woodlots are also very suitable for driving. (Photo: L. James Bashline)

This Pennsylvania buck has the flag up and will be out of sight in a moment but there is, nonetheless, that moment in which to get off a good shot. The deer was jumped by a still-hunter at the edge of a crossing. (Photo: L. James Bashline)

himself won't do well on this sort of hunt. He'd best take part in an organized drive which allows him to be more active.

The organized drive can be conducted in big woods areas, too, but it's most effective in the small patch situation where drivers and standers can be employed in an encircling way. The hunters who employ such driving methods should select a leader who knows the area well and allow him autonomy in deciding who is to do what. For a group of strangers to attempt a deer drive in unfamiliar territory is like hiring a bunch of Eskimos to serve as tour guides in Manhattan.

At a sportsmen's gathering conducted by the Pennsylvania Game Commission, Bashline admires a nontypical whitetail trophy. Heavily antlered, multitined bucks are still harvested in the Eastern woodlots, despite the increasing density of the human population. (Photo: L. James Bashline)

The standers should be posted at obvious vantage points where they can command a reasonable patch of viewing area. The drivers should be deployed to travel routes that will roust the deer out of their resting places. A drive should be well planned so each member of the party knows exactly where every other member of the group is located and from which way the drivers will approach. Conspicuous blaze-orange clothing should be worn by all. Standers and drivers must always follow the game plan and assemble at the designated spot when the drive is over. An organized drive is not the kind of hunt for the free-spirit sort. Nothing is more disgusting to a group of veteran drivers than to have one of the standers wander off on his own because he got a hunch that things were more promising at some other location. Many valuable hours of hunting time are taken up by looking for the supposedly "lost" hunter.

The free spirit who would be unwelcome in a driving group has the third option of hunting techniques and that is the still-hunt or plain old "pussyfooting." For those hunters in good physical condition and who have developed a good set of deer-spotting eyes, this is perhaps the most satisfying deer hunting available. It is best done when there is a good tracking snow and in an area where few hunters are upsetting the deer from their daily routine. In heavily hunted areas, still-hunting is difficult to

George Harrison—naturalist, photographer, writer, and field editor of *National Wildlife* magazine—poses before a Pennsylvania deer camp with a fine buck he has just brought in. (Photo: L. James Bashline)

manage when there are a lot of license-holders charging about. A stump hunter has a much better chance at the deer that the still-hunter will be tracking. The still-hunter becomes the driver for the guy who is simply waiting them out.

There are all sorts of variations on the three hunting methods listed. Which one is best? The truth is, all of them are best under certain conditions. Let's take a closer look. There is really no such thing as typical Eastern deer cover. The elusive whitetail can be found in open woods, barren fields, cedar thickets, and hemlock swamps. The terrain can be steep and. rocky, gently rolling, or flat as a table top. The method used is determined by the geography.

In thick cover such as scrub oak or conifer tangles laced with windfalls and uprooted stumps, the drive is the most productive method if your group has the area to itself. Interlocking limbs and low foliage prevent long shots and good visibility. These factors make the drive most effective if everyone follows the plan. The drivers should be spaced in such a way that each one will cover an area deer are expected to pass through. A group of five watchers and three drivers can make several half-mile drives per day and never leave a 500-acre plot. Frequently, the deer will never leave such a patch of cover. A drive should be conducted into the wind. The watchers are the ones who will usually get the shots.

In open fields and woods that are reasonably clear of understory, the stump hunter has the best chance. Deer in such areas can see the hunter approaching (although they'll probably smell him first) and the organized drive usually turns up nothing. The sit-and-watch technique is also the best way to operate on the first day of the season in areas that have a reasonably heavy concentration of hunters. A lot of the first-dayers will sit on watch for a while, but cold feet and a general nervous anticipation will put most of them on the march within an hour or two. The patient stump hunter who sits out a good stand on opening day in reasonably good deer country will almost always see deer. He may not see the buck of his dreams but the odds are good that some venison will pass his squatting place. In back-in woods situations or during the later part of the deer season when fewer hunters are afield, the still-hunter's chances become better.

The traditional New England method of taking a track on fresh snow and walking it down can be practiced everywhere that whitetails exist. It can be the toughest sort of hunt imaginable or it can end in 15 minutes. The skill of the tracker is all-important. Veteran deer trackers learned long ago that the second a wise buck knows someone is hot on his trail, the evasive action begins. Steady plodding may bring a glimpse of the buck and you may even collect the trophy but by the time you do, you could be so far into the "boonies" that dragging the venison home or to the nearest road becomes a major undertaking.

A far better trick is to weave a series of long, lazy S's that occasionally intersect the track.   As the hunter cuts the deer's prints, he may spot an ear flicking or a leg stamping and drop the buck in short order.   Keen eyes are needed for still-hunting, especially for pussyfooting through thick cover on bare ground.   With no visible tracks, the still-hunter looks for fresh signs in the form of droppings or a freshly cut twig that tells him deer are in the immediate vicinity.   A short, fast-handling rifle is important to the woods-walker.   A deer may suddenly materialize at close range and the shot must be taken in an instant or not at all.

The impressive eight- and ten-point bucks with wide spreads and long tines are the dream of every whitetail hunter.   To grow a trophy rack, a buck must be over 3½ years old and manage to find a reasonably well-balanced diet.   Some parts of the East regularly produce larger than av-erage bucks but practically anywhere east of the Mississippi can harbor a real trophy.   The big bucks are where you find them.   Maine tradition-ally turns up heavy bucks each year—some of them weighing 300 pounds. Some heavy-antlered bucks come from the flat farm country of Ohio. Even Pennsylvania and New York with their huge populations of slightly underfed deer annually record some smashers.   I have seen deep-chested bucks in the tidal marshes of Maryland.   The hunter who manages to collect a prime, well-antlered whitetail has reason to be proud.   Sheer numbers of smaller deer work against him.   Some luck, maybe a lot of it, is involved but it isn't all a matter of chance.

I lived for 31 years in what is perhaps one of the best deer regions of the United States, north-central Pennsylvania.   As a boy and later as a young adult, I spent a lot of time hunting deer there and observing the styles of other hunters.   As in all deer-hunting areas, there were some catch-as-catch-can hunters who occasionally killed a deer.   There were a few better deer stalkers who usually killed a buck.   Then there were a small handful of deer experts who always got a buck and often placed their tag on a head that was worth mounting.

One of these "lucky" ones was an ex-farmer named Howard Snyder who for several years worked for a gas company.   Howard usually ar-ranged his working hours so he could be on shift during the dark hours and out hunting during the day, an ideal arrangement for a hunter.   He owned a lever-action .300 Savage that carried a battered 2½× scope.   He hunted everything with that rifle, including turkey and squirrels.   I know, since I used to load his ammo for him.   Each year with that lever-action he nearly always downed a turkey and killed a truck load of squirrels.

I hunted with Howard on two or three occasions only, since he didn't really enjoy hunting with anyone.   It wasn't that he was unsociable, he just preferred doing things his way.   His style of stalking didn't jell with a companion, and while the buddy system suits most hunters, it didn't suit

Here's another whitetail trophy collected by the author. The deer harvested from upper New England down into the middle Atlantic states (and large parts of the Midwest) are chiefly the Northern woodland whitetail subspecies, with some interbreeding of other geographic races. Where they aren't stunted by a lack of good browse—particularly at winter yarding sites—in overpopulated areas, these are good-size deer. (Photo: L. James Bashline)

Howard. On one occasion when I talked him into letting me go along on a squirrel hunt on an oak-covered ridge, I was astounded to discover that I was soon 400 yards ahead of him. We had begun walking slowly through the woods, watching the tree tops for the telltale flop of a tail. I thought I had been moving slowly, but Howard was practically creeping. Every second step (I stopped and watched him coming through the woods), he'd stop dead-still and move his head slowly in a 300-degree arc. He searched the entire landscape from top to bottom. Once he raised his rifle carefully and shot the head off a squirrel with a reduced load from that favorite .300. Not an ideal squirrel gun in my eyes but it certainly was effective.

From later conversations with Howard and others who know about his prowess as a deer hunter, I found out that he hunted whitetails in exactly the same way. He loved the quiet snowy or, even better, rainy days when he could be relatively sure that few other hunters would be out. His notion of whitetail hunting was to do a lot of looking and move very slowly. If a movement was spotted or if he observed a patch of brown hair that seemed out of place, he would stop and wait until he ascertained what the something was or until it moved. Great patience is required for such a technique, but it works.

With a few exceptions, deer hunting in the East does not require long-range shooting. A short, easy-to-handle rifle or shotgun (some areas require the use of shotgun slugs or buckshot) with a low-powered scope or aperture sight is what's needed. The shots are usually less than 100 yards, and 50-foot shots are not at all uncommon. Large calibers that shoot ponderous projectiles and are usually classified as "brush" guns are okay if you want to stick to tradition. I prefer a bullet that moves relatively fast (above 2,700 fps) and opens up quickly. A soft-pointed bullet that opens up fast and delivers the shock inside the animal instead of passing on through seems to work out best.

I may be a bit old-fashioned in my choice of guns for whitetails but two better calibers were never designed than the old .250/3000 and the .257 Roberts. They both shoot 100-grain bullets with ample velocity and, with a chest hit, put whitetails down instantly. There's no way I'll be caught knocking the old .30/30 or .32 Special or the venerable .30/06 in 150-grain loadings. As a matter of fact, I've killed more than a dozen whitetails with the relatively modern .308 with 150-grain soft-points. But the hot .25 calibers always caught my fancy. The much newer 6mms are fine, too, with the heavier bullets.

You may have guessed by now that I don't take much stock in "brush-busting." Even though great reputations have been made by cartridges that are supposed to shoot through three laurel bushes, six oak trees, and an acre of assorted debris before knocking a whitetail sunny side up—I just don't buy it. A stick the size of a lead pencil will deflect any slug ever made and if the path isn't clear to the deer, you just ain't gonna hit him! Pick the opening and touch it off.

I wrote a magazine article a few years ago in which I took the premise that hunting whitetails could be compared with the modern shibboleth that says "football is a game of inches." Whitetail hunting is a game of seconds. There is the second when you determine that the mysterious shape ahead of you is a deer's ear. There is the second when you decide that those are antlers on the deer's head. There is the second when you decide you will attempt to shoot, and then, that micro-second that is the very best, the ultimate time, to press the trigger. Woods hunting for whitetails is exactly that: a game of important seconds. The opportunity comes fast and it's over just as quickly. The end result is, ideally, an instant kill or a clean miss.

Scoring on a whitetail in the eastern United States can be as easy as picking the morning paper out of the mail box or as difficult as finding an Arab sheik on welfare. Patience, a watchful eye, and good woodsmanship separate the lucky hunters from the license buyers. Nothing (including reading this book) can compare with experience. Go deer hunting every chance you get—even without a gun, during the off-season. If you can learn to pick out that flick of an ear with heavy foliage on the trees, you'll have a running start on tagging yourself some venison when the season opens.

10

The Great Southeastern Tradition

by Tom Brakefield

Deer season in each part of the country is a special time, one with special memories and traditions. Nowhere is this more true than in the Southeast, where I grew up and where I brought in my first venison. I had been on a stand, huddled against the cold, for several hours. Out of the corner of my eye I spotted just a hint of movement. Then another and another. Silently and miraculously four gray ghosts materialized out of the damp, soggy underbrush and began daintily moving my way. At first I thought they must be goats and had broken out of some farmer's pen. Just a lad, I made the common mistake of most novices and looked for deer (after all, they were "big" game, weren't they?) to be chest-high rather than beltbuckle-high. Most adult whitetail bucks stand somewhere between 36 and 39 inches at the shoulder.

Finally I made up my mind that these were, indeed, the long-coveted deer I had come after. As they worked their way closer to me, I made out two does and two bucks. One of the bucks was a little spike but the other was right respectable, with antlers that probably had an 18-inch spread to them.

Closer and closer they drifted and I slowly began to raise the huge old muzzle-heavy 12-gauge that seemed heavier than I was, inching it up toward the proper line of sight. I was scared stiff and my tensed muscles were shaking like Jell-O in a high wind. The big buck drifted farther away from me as he edged around the other side of a particularly thick patch of cover. But the little fellow moved closer and, just as he was about to be hidden by a particularly dense patch of undergrowth, I let fly with the No. 00 buckshot. Down he went and the brush and creepers shook as he thrashed his last. I stood there mesmerized for a moment, then I moved forward to see if my prize was actually still there. Wonder of wonders, he was, and I'll never forget the feeling of accomplishment that little spike buck gave me and the good-natured ribbing that I proudly took back at the clubhouse that evening. The warm glow of fellowship and good food during that hunt have remained with me ever afterward. Good hunts never end, not so long as we remember them, and that one typified the warmth and good times of a traditional Southern deer hunt.

Actually, the Southeast is a very large region, and deer hunting of several different types is available. Throughout any large part of the country the sport can vary considerably, depending upon terrain, traditions, densities of both hunters and game, and a number of other factors. And so it does in the South. When most hunters visualize traditional Southern hunting, they think of hunting with dogs in the lowland belt stretching across the southern portions of Georgia, Alabama, and Mississippi. This is strictly buckshot hunting, 12-gauge preferred, and the details are covered in Chapter 5 devoted to the sporting uses of dogs in deer hunting. But there are other, equally interesting aspects to Southern hunting.

Most of it is done through hunting clubs or other groups that lease prime acreage on one- to three-year contracts. This type of leased hunting is also very common in Texas, parts of Florida, and other Southern states, and I believe it will begin to show up more and more in other states in the next few years. It costs a bit of money but it gives the landowner some incentive to manage his land with the game's best interest in mind and it assures the sportsman of a place to hunt.

A hunt I made recently in southern Alabama pretty well typifies this type of deer shooting. I stayed in a rustic old cabin that had been patched and spruced up a bit to double as a clubhouse for the small club that rented the hunting rights to the land in that area. This club had thirty-two members, a bit smaller than many; on the particular weekend that I hunted with them, about forty hunters were there, including guests. We were all sleeping in Spartan but comfortable dormitory-style double bunks and it seemed that, warmed by the glow of a fire in the outsized fieldstone fireplace and a substantial bourbon-and-branchwater, I had hardly put my drink down when someone was shaking me the next morning and advising me to ''Come and git it!''

Now there are breakfasts and there are *breakfasts*. In these Deep South deer camps, eating and good fellowship rate right up on a par with the hunting itself. Two fellows were bellied up to the two stoves in the kitchen, one cooking eggs three different ways and the other frying bacon, thick slabs of country ham, and huge patties of tart country sausage. Still another fellow was making up big hoe cakes (outsized biscuits so named because in antebellum times the slaves took them to the fields to eat for lunch and heated them and the meat they placed inside on their hoe blades over an open fire).

A major element in the great Southeastern tradition is the deer-camp atmosphere of good fellowship. This is the camp of a well-organized Southern hunting club, and it obviously has most of the comforts of home. (Photo: Tom Brakefield)

The hunters were yawning and stirring and gulping scalding coffee that was strong enough to put starch into a predawn backbone. The heady kitchen aromas were enough to make the hunt worthwhile. I put away six eggs and a goodly sampling of all three meats, topped off with grits, soft and fluffy white, swimming in puddles of real butter.

After the meal we drew lots for our stand assignments (assuring fair treatment for all) and departed in 4WD vehicles for the day's drive area. Most of the vehicles had heavy-duty winches. During the late part of deer season in this area, the rains come with a vengeance. I once saw it rain nineteen days running. The land is really a gummy clay and the roads become slick and bottomless during the rains. Just walking in the soupy bog that had been the clubhouse front yard was a major chore. Often I thought the glop would actually suck off my tightly laced 8-inch hunting boots.

You have to experience this clay mud, called "gumbo" hereabouts, to believe it. As you drive along and stir it up, air is trapped within it and it snaps-crackles-and-pops with almost deafening loudness. Ahead of us, as we drove to the hunt area, I could see a big pickup begin to bind up. Mud was packing so tightly to the wheels that it was binding them in

Deer season is the rainy season in large parts of the sparsely settled backcountry in the South. Mud and washouts can be a big problem. Here, a 4WD vehicle helps a similar vehicle out by means of a winch. Winch-equipped 4WD's are every bit as valuable in this kind of deer country as in rough Western terrain. (Photo: Tom Brakefield)

the wheel wells and, although the gunk never got to the point of stopping the truck cold, this often can happen. When this goo dries out, it has a Rockwell rating of something over 60C in hardness and you can easily injure your foot by trying to kick chunks of it off the bumpers or wheels.

The roads become so bad because this is flat, piney-woods country with generally poor drainage and you have to stick to the gouged-out super-slick ruts that pass for roads rather than driving to the side on the edges of the grassy fields where the traction is considerably better. The local landowner who leases the hunting rights raises cattle and soybeans as do most other farmers in this area, and if the hunters drive off the roads their vehicles quickly chew up valuable cropland or grass for cattle forage. Good hunter–landowner relations are an absolute must (as they are in any type of hunting anywhere) so one of the club's basic rules, enforced by severe fines when necessary, is to never leave the road with a vehicle.

The club's two parcels of leased hunting land run 2,000 and 1,200 acres. The club is financed by $100 annual dues, chipped in by the members at the first of each year, plus any fines that are levied and collected for rule

At a Southern deer camp, hunters and their wives are pictured during the leisurely break between morning and afternoon hunts. Lunch in this instance was a heaping bowl of mulligan stew, with venison as the chief ingredient. (Photo: Tom Brakefield)

infractions. The recent cost has been 25¢ per acre per year for the hunting rights on a three-year contract. However, the costs of hunting are increasing in Alabama just as they are elsewhere. When the current contract is up, there are dire predictions that only one-year contracts will be available and that the cost will zoom first to 50¢ per acre and then up to $1 in the reasonably near future. But considering that this is a game-rich area and the club has exclusive hunting rights, and also the fact that the landowner is encouraged to plant certain spots with deer food and/or leave some of his basic crop standing for them, it's still a pretty good deal.

The hunters learn their leased area minutely. Eventually they come to know every wrinkle and hollow in the sizable acreages about as intimately as the deer do. Aerial photo maps and topo maps are posted in the clubhouse and records are kept of kill sites and dates as well as drive dates and exact stand sites. Thus, over a period of time, rather exact data are available to help hunters plan better hunts or adjust stand locations as

needed.   There is more to this type of hunting than just releasing some
dogs and hoping that a deer runs by.

This low, flat, marshy land that comprises roughly the southern 40 or 50
percent of Alabama, Georgia, and Mississippi is the "dog-hunting belt" of
the South.   Immediately to the north is another zone, roughly 100 to 250
miles deep, depending upon the spot, where the low coastal plain begins to
hump up into the more rolling piedmont area.   Here smaller mixed-crop
farms are more in evidence.   The cover isn't quite as thick and more of
the land has been cleared, though large wooded acreages owned by paper
companies can still be found.   Drainage is better, so access by 2WD
vehicles is much more feasible during the rainy season.

In this area, clubs with leased hunting rights are somewhat less common
and the individual or informal group is more commonly seen.   Though
buckshot, slugs, and centerfire rifles are all legal in most of this area, the
slug is probably the most commonly used ammunition.   Ranges can be a
bit long for buckshot and often the cover isn't quite heavy enough to
warrant its use.   Yet this area is still reasonably flat and, for this part of
the country, relatively densely populated.   Much of the best hunting is in
rather civilized areas around the edges of the small to medium farms.

After all the attending members of a hunting club have drawn their stand
assignments, the huntmaster goes over the morning's or afternoon's plan with
them, explaining all details of the driving procedure, and then leads them
out.   Here, a huntmaster in Alabama (facing right) tells a hunter this is the
place for him to drop out of line and take his stand.   (Photo: Tom Brakefield)

Thus, the common use of the 12-gauge rifled slug. However, there is great variety in Southeastern hunting conditions, and rifles are used effectively in many spots.

Still farther north, beginning in the top portions of these three states and moving into Tennessee and Kentucky, the piedmont continues to build up into some respectable ridges and hills—"mountains" by Eastern standards. Some are pretty steep and rough, and reminiscent of deer stalking in the Adirondacks or the Catskills or the mountains of Pennsylvania.

Large valleys and lowland farming areas are dotted all through this higher, rougher zone but, to one degree or another, hill hunting is generally the most commonly encountered hunting. Many visitors are amazed, in fact, at just how rugged and wild the northern portions of Alabama and Georgia are in certain spots, not to mention eastern Tennessee, western North Carolina, and various areas throughout Kentucky and Virginia. Here the centerfire rifle is king, with newer calibers edging out the old reliable "thutty-thutty" carbines.

The .308 has found much favor here and a surprising number of .243 Winchesters and 6mm Remingtons are seen. Many hunters want a flat-shooting rifle of the .243–.270 persuasion that they can also use on mule deer and pronghorn out West. Also, there can be an occasional long shot here on a power line right of way or across from one hill to another. Scopes are seen on the vast majority of rifles, even the .30/30s and other rainbow-arced "brush busters."

It's my impression that the vast majority of younger hunters coming up in this area do not place a lot of credibility on the brush-busting capabilities of these older, low-velocity and big-caliber slugs. They may help penetrate brush a tad better in certain very specialized circumstances (such as hitting a twig immediately in front of the deer and then hitting him because the bullet ricocheted at a somewhat less acute angle) but apparently the greater number of hunters opt for the flatter-shooting shells, believing that they gain more than they give up by doing so. I am in agreement.

Southern deer hunting is rich in tradition and history, and the hunting is good. Most sportsmen from other regions are astonished when they learn the size of the deer herds here and the length of the seasons and generosity of the bag limits. Even in parts of the North, deer herds occasionally require thinning because of reduced habitat, and experts question whether the bucks-only laws in some instances aren't an unnecessary, archaic, even harmful kind of chivalry. In stipulated portions of some Southern states, antlerless deer are legal game; often several days of the regular season are open for antlerless deer on a state-wide basis. True, a number of states in other parts of the country have been experimenting with the same approach, but if you care more about good venison than about a rack on your wall you'll do well to inquire about the legal taking of does in a state like Alabama.   As for bucks, the limit there is mentioned in Chapter 5 and it's worth repeating here.   The limit is one.   No, not one per season—one per day!   One per day for three months, because that's how long the season lasts, and the deer are most definitely not being overharvested.

More out-of-state hunters should trek south for a deer-hunting vacation, and this can usually be arranged after the home deer season is over. Also, though the weather can be a bit brisk (especially when you remain motionless for several hours on a stand) it is warm indeed when compared with the chilling temperatures in the North—a welcome break in the winter cold for Northern visitors.   Southern hospitality still reigns supreme, and even though professional hunting guides and outfitters are almost unknown in this region, a stranger can usually make a connection by calling or writing the state fish and game commissions for leads.

This man has drawn a stand in thick, brushy, picket-post woods, but there is a reasonably open crossing in front of him and he may get a good shot at any deer moved his way by the drivers—whether or not they're using dogs on this particular hunt.   (Photo: Tom Brakefield)

A driven Virginia whitetail moves across a fairly open wooded flat. He's loping along at fair speed, but is close enough—and offers a fully exposed broadside target, at that—for a clean one-shot kill.

The authorities can often give you the names of some hunting clubs and information as to how to contact their officers or the names of some of the small towns in the midst of the richest deer-hunting areas. It's then a simple matter to contact the local chambers of commerce or mayors of these towns with requests that they put you in touch with someone who might be able to help you set up a hunt. Some farmers or ranchers would be happy to work with you for a modest fee, and many hunting clubs, if they sense you're a good guy and ardent deer hunter, will be glad to welcome you as a guest for a long weekend of hunting just so they can swap tall tales and deer lore with another hunter from a different region. Often exchange hunts—whereby a Southern hunter visits you the following year—can be arranged and this is a good way to form new friendships as well as expand your hunting horizons.

How to Buck the Midwest

by Erwin A. Bauer

During the late 1960s, my old friend Lew Baker established a record which would be difficult, perhaps impossible, to match anymore. Early on the mornings of four consecutive opening days, he bagged extremely good bucks. Except that Lew missed a hard shot during a blinding snow squall, he might have made it five in a row. But what, it's fair to ask, is so extraordinary about that?

To begin, Lew was hunting in Ohio, a state where the deer herd is not large and where (on the average) only one hunter in every twelve bags any kind of deer at all. Only about 25 percent even have a shot at deer. Some years, success is even lower than that. Therefore the odds of getting a fine buck on four first days in a row are about 10,000 to one—like pitching two no-hitters in both ends of a big league baseball doubleheader.

What is even more remarkable is that my friend didn't use any deep, dark, or illegal techniques to score. He hunted on unposted land open to the public and took his chances along with the multitudes of other eager sportsmen in the state. It's true that Lew was a very experienced outdoorsman and that is always a great factor in any gunner's favor. His secret (if it can be called that) was just to plan ahead and to hunt the way everyone should proceed under the circumstances. It is also the best formula for hunting whitetails almost anywhere in the Midwest—that belt stretching from Ohio westward to Missouri and from the Ohio River northward to Minnesota. Throw in Kentucky for good measure since it is more similar to the Midwest geographically than it is to the South.

This is a region of mixed habitats. The Southern part is either entirely agricultural or partly so, being punctuated by hardwood forests, second-growth hillsides, and strips of bottomland brush or timber along many waterways. The farther north you travel into the Midwest, the more the farming lands evaporate into Northern evergreen forests. Taken on the average, the portions that might be called ideal deer cover are neither as lush nor as dense as whitetail country in the Southeast, nor as open generally as the muley country of the Western mountains.

But an interesting evolution has taken place in many parts of the Midwest. Here the once woodland whitetail has somewhat adapted to farmland living—at least to thriving and growing heavy along the fringes of cultivation. All at once during the past few decades, cornfed venison has become available from cornfed bucks that grow much bigger than their cousins of the spruce and balsam swamps. Now suddenly there is at least limited deer hunting where none existed before. And true or not, a good many hunters are convinced that living off the fat of the land has also made the grainfield whitetails a lot wiser. Maybe they have to be to cope—to survive—in a more open environment within sight of silos and cattle compounds.

Now back to Lew Baker. The first thing Lew did was to know and locate local deer—intimately. The next thing, the clincher, was to hunt them by the best, most deadly (and legal) method possible in that area.

For at least a week and usually longer before opening day, Lew went scouting. The day the season begins, he correctly reasoned, is much too late to start looking for whitetails unless you simply enjoy being baffled and outwitted. So consider, as Lew did, the following vital points.

Whitetails go largely unmolested during most of the year, but their quiet daily routines are suddenly disrupted early on opening day when the hunters hit the woods. The bulk of the kill is made on opening day, and the number of deer taken declines rapidly thereafter as each day of the season passes.

Deer behavior changes abruptly from normal to abnormal, and finding the animals becomes increasingly difficult. Old bucks become especially unpredictable and elusive. They actually seem to vanish from the earth. So the hunter with the best chance of success is the one waiting in the best possible position at daybreak on opening day. And only preseason scouting can locate that right place. Hunting groups that make big drives often benefit from the preseason scouting, too.

Assume that you are an enthusiastic deer hunter and have set aside a week or so of your annual vacation time for deer hunting. A recent survey in several Midwestern states revealed that the average deer hunter spent 3½ days in the woods, although he may have intended to spend a week or more. More significantly, most of those surveyed hunted on the first 3½ days of the season.

Instead of scheduling vacation time to begin with opening day as most men do, why not go early and spend several days scouting before the other hunters hit the heavy cover? That way, you get the jump on them as well as on the deer.

Preseason scouting has a fascination all its own. You're not under any great pressure, and buck fever isn't a factor. So you'll probably be a better observer, and you'll learn more about whitetails than you would if you were carrying a firearm. When you're reconnoitering on foot, you can also brush up on your woodsmanship—trying to walk more quietly, for instance.

In some states it is perfectly legal to combine some form of hunting with preseason scouting before the firearms deer season. For example, the archery deer season may immediately precede the firearms season. In such circumstances you could be bowhunting while you look for a deer to take with your rifle later on. Elsewhere the season on such species as ruffed grouse and snowshoe hares may be open, and that also provides an opportunity to double up. But because of the shooting involved in upland gunning and the concentration it requires, it isn't as helpful as bowhunting. You won't spot deer so often if you're blasting noisily away at birds.

In some regions that are crisscrossed by many roads, the bulk of the scouting can be done by car. In rough country, a 4WD vehicle is a great help. It is wise to get a county map, available in almost every county

This hunter is visibly tired, sweating with exertion, but he's a satisfied man. His buck is an unusually big Minnesota buck with five long, thick tines on each of the main beams. (Photo: Norm Nelson)

courthouse, or if you're hunting in a national forest, a forest map available at regional headquarters and most ranger stations. Large-scale topo sheets may also be very helpful.

Sighting the animals themselves is obviously the best possible evidence. But in some areas, especially when the weather is very mild, deer may not move about much until after dark. So you may have to rely on tracks and other testimony.

Fresh tracks are a good indication that deer are in the area. Keep an eye out for fresh pellets, pawings in the earth, and rubs on saplings and trees. Rubs are easy to spot. They are made just before and during the rut by bucks that are scraping the velvet off their antlers. That rubbing often peels off the bark, leaving a bare spot that is noticeable from a distance. You'll often find the ground pawed up nearby.

Another preseason scouting method is to drive about at night and use a spotlight to locate deer. Their eyes show up clearly when the artificial light hits them, and you can often see antlers, too. Never carry both a spotlight *and any kind of firearm* in your car at the same time at night. Having both during darkness is usually considered to be good evidence of deer jacking—illegal everywhere. Whenever I have gone out at night with a spotlight, I've always informed the local game warden or forest ranger beforehand about what I was going to do, so that there could be no mistake.

Small areas are best scouted by simply hiking across them, perhaps once from north to south and then from east to west. Two or more hunters hiking on parallel paths can inspect an area even more thoroughly. Although the hikers should certainly take note of actual sightings, a man afoot usually must depend heavily on the fresh sign he finds along his route.

There are many places in the Midwest and southern Canada where a canoe float trip or a slow cruise around the edge of a lake can reveal a great deal. Tracks on sandy or muddy beaches are easy to spot. Preseason scouting for whitetails is productive because going afield early can make you a better, more confident hunter. You're more likely to succeed when you have confidence and are familiar with your surroundings. It's a simple matter of psychology.

If you know where the deer are on opening morning, you are sure of yourself, so you're much more likely to hunt skillfully and shoot well.

And if all the camp chores are done and you have enjoyed a good night's sleep, you're even more likely to do your best. Going out on a hard day's hunt relaxed and refreshed means more than most hunters realize. Any hunter needs every small advantage he can muster when the whitetail buck is the game.

Yet scouting alone will not put a Midwest buck in the freezer or a trophy

This Missouri buck has just detected an alien presence. He's not quite sure yet if it's a human intruder, but in a split second he'll make for cover on the wooded ridge in the background. This sort of hilly hardwood forest, interspersed with brush and farmland, is typical. Hunting pressure is sometimes heavy, but the bucks are often big—and with advance planning there's a good chance of success. (Photo: Missouri Dept. of Conservation)

rack on the wall. You still have to apply the scouting information obtained to proper use in the field. An extremely important survey completed in 1974 by John Cartier, Midwestern field editor of *Outdoor Life,* suggests how to do exactly that.

Cartier contacted the fish and game departments of all states to find out how deer are killed across the country. As anyone might guess, techniques vary greatly from region to region and are dictated by the geography, by the vegetation types which are common, by the number and species of deer. But hunting pressure is extremely important, too, and at least in the Midwest may be the most important consideration of all.

Consider these figures compiled by Cartier. In the Midwestern states only 11 percent of the deer killed are taken by still-hunting and 7.5 percent by stalking. Driving accounts for 28.8 percent of all whitetails harvested.

The most significant statistic is that over half (53.5 percent) of all deer are taken from stands.   Digging a little deeper, we can safely assume that still-hunting and stalking percentages are as high as they are because they work better in the evergreen forests of the North.   At the same time, the percentage for standing success would be greater if only the most heavily populated states—the agricultural belt (where hunting is most concentrated in isolated spots)—had been censused.   Cartier learned that an incredible 95 percent of all deer shot in Missouri were taken by hunters waiting on a stand.

We have already pointed out that the great, sudden invasion of deer habitat by hunters on opening morning creates a general confusion among

A Michigan buck, with a doe and fawn, peers from a thicket of brush and saplings.   Cover like this, where clear shots are infrequent except at close range, will often be found punctuating big stands of coniferous woods.   Some of the timber, which provided good second-growth browse and cover for many years after the era of big logging operations, has now grown into mature forest that's less beneficial for deer.   But management techniques have improved and the outlook is brightening.   (Photo: Michigan Dept. of Conservation)

hunters and hunted alike. Initially deer will try to escape the crunch by following old familiar runways, along which the really wise deer hunter (like Lew Baker) will be waiting at dawn's first light. Even after that first barrage, a patient, well-concealed stander has the best possible advantage because the army of hunters will keep the deer circulating. There's a good chance that eventually one will move within good gunshot range of the stander, even if he isn't in the best possible position.

Let's face some other facts. Most deer hunters in the woods today are relatively inexperienced and in no way a match for whitetails, which have keenly developed senses. An old buck's eyesight is only remarkable. Therefore an inexperienced hunter's best bet, bar none, is to find a hidden spot and to stay motionless there. That way he will be most inconspicuous to alert, nervous deer. In much of the Midwest any hunter's chances for scoring are in direct ratio to how well he blends into his background and how many other hunters are milling about in the area.

Of course, considerable skill is involved in standing, a subject considered in more detail elsewhere in this book. Let's just list a few basics here. The stander should select a comfortable spot because that way he can better remain entirely motionless for long periods. He should have a good field of fire all around and not have his vision badly obscured by foliage or the terrain. It is always a considerable advantage to be above the deer, as in a tree blind, but some states have regulations governing the use and building of such structures. In Minnesota, for instance, there is a limit on height. Be sure to check thoroughly the limitations or laws wherever you plan to hunt.

Now only one more crucial item remains. You've picked your stand properly and a big buck is on the way. He may be strolling closer, cautiously making short steps at a time, while buck fever unsteadies your posture. Or he may be pounding pell-mell head on. Either way, you have to put him down to stay.

Missed shots at vanishing whitetails are as common as red wool shirts during the deer season. If shirttails actually were cut off every time somebody blew a shot at a buck, America's shirtmakers wouldn't be able to keep up with the demand.

No statistics exist to prove it, but I'm sure that the number of shots fired for each animal taken is greater with whitetail bucks than it is with any other big-game animal. That claim is certainly true in my own experience, and every other veteran big-game hunter with whom I discussed the matter says the same thing. Why are so many whitetails missed, and what can you do to improve your score?

First, let's consider the quarry. The mature whitetail buck is an extraordinary animal. He is as tough and tenacious of life as he is handsome. A buck that has survived several hunting seasons as well as brutal winters has been honed sharp by danger and hardship. He is not the fastest animal on four feet, but I believe he can reach his top speed more quickly than any other animal of similar size.

The whitetail's vision, excellent hearing, and superb scenting ability have been thoroughly described in hunting literature, and the wise whitetail takes full advantage of the environment in which he lives. The forests of mixed hardwood and evergreen, the swamps and second-growth thickets, the laurel and honeysuckle tangles are perfect for the deer, but not for the deer hunter. When you consider typical Midwest habitat and the whitetail's ability to race through it at high speed or seemingly vanish in the cover, you know you are hunting an animal that was made to be missed.

Most deer hunters add to their troubles because they only dust off the old shooting iron once a year. Misses are to be expected if you don't shoot much, but even very experienced hunters and marksmen miss whitetails, too. Few men can honestly say that they always connect. In his excellent book *The Hunting Rifle,* Jack O'Connor admits that he has missed more deer in the brush than anywhere else.

Too many deer hunters do not use the best firearm for the purpose. There are two types of deer rifle—one for short-range use in brush or forest, the other for shooting in open or hilly country. The long-range rifle is used mostly for hunting mule deer out West. The ideal brush rifle for whitetails should be light, should be fast to operate, and should have a short barrel chambered for a cartridge with a fairly heavy bullet traveling at moderate velocity.

It's obvious that the whitetail hunter must be able to get on target fast, not unlike a scattergunner swinging on a flushed bird. With whitetails, you seldom have time to squeeze off a shot at a stationary target from a rest. When spotted, two out of three bucks are already in motion, and the third soon will be.

Another reason for using a brush rifle and heavy bullets is the matter of getting through Midwestern brush to reach the target. Any bullet can be deflected by brush, but the deflection is far greater with light, high-velocity, sharp-pointed bullets. I have killed two whitetails with 180-grain bullets from a .30/06 that cut off twigs and a sapling on the way. Although there's no question about the superiority of a bolt-action for certain uses, lever-action, pump-action, and semi-automatic rifles are popular for whitetail hunting because they are faster to use than a bolt-action rifle. In the brush, a second or sometimes even a third shot can be very useful, but you must get them off before the deer vanishes.

The rifle you select may well depend on your preference regarding a combination of caliber and action—lever, pump, or auto—as well as the design, weight, handling qualities, price, and various features available

In the Midwest, as elsewhere, the difficulties of still-hunting carry their own rewards. Only a still-hunter—and a proficient one, at that—is likely ever to surprise a bedded buck like this fine Illinois specimen. (Photo: Illinois Dept. of Conservation)

among the many hunting models.   In Chapter 1 on firearms, Dave Petzal goes into greater detail.   Bear in mind as you ponder his advice that good, fast, reliable repeaters of one kind or another are chambered for such cartridges as the .30/06, the .308 Winchester, .35 Remington, .44 Magnum, and .444 Marlin.   For open country I might suggest some other calibers (and a bolt-action) but all of these have taken plenty of whitetails in brush and timber.   Do veteran riflemen ever disagree about such matters?   Of course.   That's part of what makes the sport so interesting.   Read Dave Petzal's chapter, weigh his observations, mine, and those of the other contributors against the conditions you've encountered yourself, and then decide what's right for you.

In a number of Midwestern (and Eastern) states, deer hunters are required by law to use smoothbores and rifled slugs instead of rifles because rifles carry too far for use in densely populated areas.   When used at close ranges in brush, the 12-gauge shotgun slug is extremely effective.   It is practical to mount a peep sight or a scope on most shotguns.   For many years I used a pump shotgun with a 20-inch improved-cylinder barrel, designed especially for rifled slugs.   On it is mounted a 2½× Weaver scope.   The gun has accounted for lots of deer.

Rifle sights for brush hunting cause many arguments among deer hunters.   Open iron sights may be best for a hunter who remains fairly calm when he gets a shot, but an excitable hunter has a tendency to hold high and shoot over the target when he's using a notch rear sight. Peep sights suit some shooters very well, and with them there's no built-in tendency to shoot high. For the average whitetail hunter, however, a low-power scope, say 1× to 2½×, is the best possible sight for whitetails in the woods. Low-power scopes have a wide field of view, which makes it possible to pick up the target quickly. A magnifying sight also makes it easier to pick out detail—to distinguish deerhide against a brushy background and spot antlers.

On the other hand, rain or snow can be a severe handicap to the man who uses a scope. Rain or snow can block vision, and no scope cover or protector has yet been designed that can be removed fast enough to permit a shot at an alert buck through a Northern forest. My own feeling is that quick-detachable and swing-off scope mounts aren't much help. If you suddenly get a shot and find that your scope is fogged or clogged, it takes too much time to get the scope out of the way, and sometimes these mounts freeze up. Some hunters, however, manage very well with them. To complicate things still more, many shots at whitetails come very early and very late in the day, when the light is poorest. Long shadows and dim light give the deer one more advantage.

Using the best possible rifle will not guarantee venison in the freezer. The hunter must know how to shoot it accurately and quickly, and that takes a lot of practice. The hunter must also learn to aim at a particular part of the deer—not the whole deer. The best aiming point is the heart-lung area just behind the front legs. A hit anywhere in that area will eventually drop any deer if it does not do so instantaneously. If the animal is not standing or running broadside, the shot should still be aimed to reach the forepart of the rib cage by quartering into it from the rear or driving forward between the hams.

Today the future of Midwestern whitetail deer and deer hunting appears fairly bright. The herds, although not increasing, seem to be stabilized and are well managed by game biologists. The numbers of hunters—hunting pressure—can be regulated carefully. Without question the threat to a great sport · is coming from uncontrolled sprawl and development—the destruction of habitat—far out across the beautiful Midwestern landscape. Unsound forestry management, which the Forest Service suddenly seems to endorse in too many woodlands, could also greatly diminish deer herds.

Over most of the Midwest, the prosperity of deer offers an unfailing index of the quality of life in general. If we lose the deer, and the sport they provide, we may have lost far more than delicious venison dinners.

12

Tower-Sitting, Rattling, and Other Southwestern Strategies

by Byron W. Dalrymple

When one speaks of hunting whitetail deer in the "Southwest," the term means chiefly Texas. The other states involved are Oklahoma, New Mexico, and Arizona, but it is Texas that has most of the deer. This largest of the contiguous states is an enormous expanse of country, just over 267,000 square miles, and it has a phenomenal whitetail herd.

It is estimated, in fact, that at least one-fifth of all the whitetails in the nation are in Lone Star country, a state population of some 3½ million head. The harvest in typically good years surpasses 350,000, an astonishing number, especially on a continuing basis. That is more than the total taken in all of New England plus New York, New Jersey, Pennsylvania, and all of the East Coast states combined.

To anyone living east of the Mississippi, some of the hunting habitat would seem strange, indeed. I remember with wry amusement my introduction, for example, to what is locally called the Brush Country in southern Texas. This is the region beginning roughly one tier of counties south of San Antonio, and fanning out on the west toward Eagle Pass, southeastward toward George West, and running south to the Mexican border, with a hub at Laredo.

The Brush Country counties contain the largest whitetails in Texas. Like the majority of Texas whitetails, these are the subspecies *texanus,* but something about the habitat turns out deer much larger than elsewhere in the state. In the last edition of the record book, Texas was represented with thirty-nine, all but a couple of them taken from this southern area.

At any rate, my first visit to the region, about 25 years ago, was not for deer (the season was over) but for javelina. When I saw the gently rolling, arid terrain, an endless sweep of dense thornbrush and cactus, with few large trees except here and there a clump of ancient mesquites, I thought it the most barren hunk of real estate I had ever looked at.   During the javelina hunt, I was startled witless when I jumped an enormous whitetail buck from a thicket.   The time was January and the bucks still had their antlers.

I'd not given a thought to deer.   It seemed an impossible country for them.   Before the hunt wound up, however, I had seen several more and I was already making plans to go deer hunting there.   Not long afterward we moved permanently to Texas and I have hunted the brush many times.   I have hunted deer in many states, but the largest whitetails I have ever seen and shot have been there.

The whitetail deer has proved to be one of the best colonizers of all our big-game animals.   It has adapted to an amazing variety of terrain.   Nowhere is this more vividly illustrated than in the Southwest.   You can hunt in the piney woods of East Texas in areas reminiscent of southern Georgia or northern Florida.   In portions of eastern Oklahoma, you literally hunt in the Ozarks, the tail end of those mountains.   Elsewhere in Oklahoma there are big, fat deer keeping their private lives supremely private in farm-country woodlots.   On the western fringe of the Texas Brush Country—for example, in the Devil's River region of Val Verde County—there are rugged, low mountains that look for all the world like the domain of desert mule deer, but actually teem with whitetails of husky dimensions.   In the Texas Hill Country, in the south-central part of the state, the hunting is among live oaks, Spanish oaks, and Ashe juniper, in most scenic settings, with brushy, steep canyons through which flow small crystal streams.   In southwestern New Mexico and southeastern Arizona the prime whitetail country is up in the grass and oak vegetation zone of the mountain ranges at about 6,000 feet.   Thus, one of the unique features of Southwestern whitetail hunting is that you can take your pick of a wide variety of hunting country.

It will be useful to prospective hunters first to get a clear picture of where the deer are in the Southwest.   In Oklahoma, whitetails are found in all 77 counties but the preponderance of the herd is in the east.   The southeastern counties rate highest, but east-central and northeast also rate high.   Westward, in general, the heaviest concentrations follow the large river courses and their tributaries—the Cimarron, North and South Canadian, Washita.

Oklahoma is fortunate in having numerous tracts owned by the state, where hunting is fair to good.   There are also two large blocks of the Ouachita National Forest in the southeast, plus scattered expanses of national grasslands in the west.   The McAlester Naval Ammunition Depot has some of the best hunting, by permit, in the state.   Permission to hunt on private lands is still not especially difficult to obtain in Oklahoma.

In Texas, whitetails range throughout the state. There are excellent opportunities in the eastern and northern counties, in the Panhandle, and even in parts of the lower desert-mountain country of far-west Texas. But the heaviest whitetail concentration is on the Edwards Plateau, which takes in most of the south-central area of the state and

If you've never seen a truly stunning whitetail rack, have a close look at this massively beamed set of antlers on a Texas buck in the Brush Country. Almost all of the record-book Texas whitetails have come from this region—a few counties ranging from south of San Antonio to the border. (Photo: Byron W. Dalrymple)

spreads westward along and north of the Rio Grande. Within this broad region, the so-called Hill Country encompassing the counties west and northwest of San Antonio has the most deer, just possibly the heaviest whitetail concentration on the continent.

The size of these deer varies county to county. They are relatively small, by no means as large as those to the south, in the Brush Country. There the deer are numerous, but less so than in the Hill Country. The two areas cover the best whitetail hunting in the state.

Far to the west, across the Pecos River in Brewster and Presidio counties, there is a very small, handsome whitetail often mistaken for the Arizona whitetail or Coues deer. It is the subspecies *carminis,* the Carmen Mountains whitetail. It dwells, in sparse population currently estimated at possibly 1,500 animals, in the high portions of small mountain ranges in the Big Bend region. This sprightly deer, which I have had opportunity to hunt and collect several times, lives in the piñon, oak, and madrona cover, usually from about 5,000 feet on up to the top of the mountains that rise from a desert floor. The larger Texas (*texanus*) whitetails are found in modest numbers in the foothills.

It is not finding the deer, but finding a place to hunt that poses some problems in Texas. There is very little public land—some national forest tracts north of Houston, some national grasslands in the Panhandle, a scattering of timber-company lands in the east that allow hunting, and a very modest amount on state-owned game-management units, with hunting regulated by drawings. Otherwise, Texas deer hunting is strictly for fees. There are three chief arrangements: day hunting at so much per day, most of it on small ranches in the Hill Country; lease hunting, common throughout the state, wherein an individual or group will lease hunting rights on a specified acreage for a season or for several years; and package hunts, on which a rancher furnishes guide and transport for a hunt of a specified length. On some of these, meals and lodging are also available, at stipulated prices. A few package-hunt ranches offer guaranteed hunts—no deer, no pay.

Thus, unless you own land or have a friend who does, you generally have to pay to hunt deer in Texas. Although all types of hunting are getting more and more expensive, there are advantages to the fee system. On a well-run day hunt, only a given number of hunters is assigned to any pasture. On a lease, no one is there but the lessees. On a package hunt, the success rate is usually 100 percent and there is no crowding, usually only a single party in any one pasture at a given time.

The usual procedure for finding a place to hunt in Texas is to contact chambers of commerce in the area where you wish to go. Many landowners who need hunters are listed with the chambers of commerce. Or you might place a preseason ad in a local daily or weekly, stating how many hunters you have and what type of hunt you want.   A few large ranches, such as the well-known YO Ranch near Mountain Home and Dolan Creek Ranch on Devil's River, advertise nationally in outdoor magazines.   These and others like them offer package hunts.

Getting a lease or a package or day hunt nowadays in the Brush Coun-

The elevated stand, or tower, assumes several different guises in the Southwest.   Here's a hunting car mounted with a platform and chairs for two hunters.   From this vantage point they can see far out over the open terrain and spot deer in clumps of low cover.   They can also rattle them up surprisingly close to their exposed position if they remain quiet and don't move much except to do the rattling.   The author is seated at left, rattling the antlers.

Here's a permanent tower blind in the Texas Hill Country. For safety's sake, the hunter preferred not to encumber himself with his rifle while ascending the ladder. Instead, he left it at the bottom, tied to a rope by which he can now retrieve it. These blinds tend to be in exposed positions offering a wide view. They're accepted by the deer as a permanent part of the landscape, so they don't spook game.

try is chancy. Leases are long, with dozens of takers in line. The Hill Country in general offers the best opportunity for visitors. So far as the little Carmen Mountains deer are concerned, all are on huge ranches of fifty-thousand to a quarter-million acres, and this is basically desert muley country. The season is brief and the ranches are mostly booked full with mule-deer hunters. It's every man for himself in lining up a hunt. In fact, it's pretty much that way throughout Texas, yet success is so high that it's worthwhile to ferret out a place, and with a little persistence it can be done.

This photo was taken shortly after dawn in the Texas Brush Country. Look closely into the dark brush in front of the hunter's rifle, and you'll see the head of a good buck that was called in by the rattling technique. The sportsman at right is gripping the antlers in the correct manner for rattling.

There is not much whitetail hunting in New Mexico. A scattering of Texas whitetails is found in the Lincoln National Forest in south-central-southern New Mexico, a few west of Raton, and a very few (possibly another subspecies) in the sandhills and brushy draws on several eastern counties. In the extreme southwest, mainly in the Animas and Peloncillo Mountains, there is a fair population of the handsome and sporty Coues, or Arizona, whitetail. The total New Mexico whitetail population is probably no more than 10,000.

Most of the Coues deer are found in southern Arizona. Although this small whitetail subspecies ranges in suitable terrain across most of the southern half of the state, and is the only whitetail in Arizona, the preponderance of the population is in the various mountain ranges of the Southeast. Some of the better ranges include the Santa Ritas, Catalinas, Huachucas, Grahams, Galiuros, Santa Teresas, Tumacacoris, and Chiricahuas. An average annual whitetail kill in Arizona runs about 3,000, possibly a sixth or less of the state's total deer harvest. The others, of course, are mule deer. In both Arizona and New Mexico there is no problem finding places to hunt. There are vast acreages of national forest and other public lands.

Most Southwestern deer hunting is done by the standard methods of still-hunting or stand-hunting. Deer drives, except for a casual small attempt here and there to push deer out of a cedar brake, are all but unknown. There are, however, some unique methods used in Texas that apparently originated there and that are not used to any extent elsewhere across the country. One is the tower or high blind. Nonresidents have spoken of them as "high sits" (a term derived from the German), although I've never heard a Texan use the term. In fact, in the Hill Country where hundreds of gunners hunt this way, everyone knows that when you speak of a "deer blind" you don't mean one on the ground but one high above.

On many ranches these so-called towers take the form of small buildings on stilts. My first deer hunting in Texas, as I recall with some amusement because I could hardly believe it, was done from one of these permanent installations. I was dropped off at dawn by my host and told I'd be picked up at nine-thirty. I climbed a ladder, pushed up a trap door, entered a snug little room about six by six. There were sliding windows on three sides, a comfortable chair, a bottle of water, and a roll of toilet paper. There was even a small sand bag for a rest to be placed on the window sill. Shooting avenues had been cleared in the cedar and live oak so crossing deer could be seen.

The basic idea, of course, is that deer seldom look up, and the hunter has an excellent view plus comfort. Many ranchers use these permanent stands, which also keep visiting hunters from walking and possibly endangering one another. Some have a rule that you stay in your stand until picked up—except, of course, to gut a kill.

Down in the Brush Country, towers of this sort are usually not as plush. Some are rather rickety open boxes attached to a tall upright of telephone-pole size. Hundreds of portable tower stands are also in use, and building them is a big business in Texas. Most of these have a steel tripod frame, atop which is affixed a swivel seat with a circular footrest. Some are topped with small enclosed or partially enclosed blinds. If you enjoy this kind of hunting, such stands are extremely productive in the dense cactus and thornbrush. From ground level you can't see into it, and most of it is high enough so deer don't show above it. A high view gives the hunter a chance to see deer moving at close range or distantly.

Most interesting and dramatic of Texas hunting methods is rattling antlers during the rut. Although rattling has been used in other places across the country, it supposedly originated in the dense thornbrush of the border country in Texas, and most of it is still done in Texas. For those who have never seen it, the results are all but unbelievable.

While producing a film a few years ago, I had a cameraman partner who was from Michigan. He had heard of rattling but I could tell he really didn't put much stock in it. Just after dawn on the first morning, I parked my 4WD, got my rattling "horns," and beckoned him to follow me. With movie camera mounted on a gunstock, he did so. We walked quietly into the cover for possibly 100 yards. There was a small opening here. I backed up into a cedar thicket, he got set behind me, and I began rattling.

At the first clash of the antlers there was a clatter of stones. A big 10-pointer barreled into the opening. Eyes wild, nostrils flared, he came tearing straight at us. He slid to a stop not 10 feet away, staring, confused. Then he whirled and ran. I tickled the antlers together and darned if he didn't wheel and come back. Meanwhile I realized I wasn't hearing the whir of the camera. I looked around. The cameraman was sitting with eyes wide, staring. In his amazement he had forgotten to run this superb footage!

Rattling is effective only during the rut, but that may be a period of a month or more. It is really a simple routine. To fix up a set of rattling antlers, saw them individually from the skull. I like an eight-point set, including brow tines, which I saw off. I leave the burl on the base of each antler, but if they bother your hands, cut them off, too. Smooth down the saw cuts with a file. If the antler points are especially sharp, trim and file them so they won't hurt your hands. Drill a hole in each antler base if you've cut off the burls, so you can tie a thong between them and sling the set over your shoulder for carrying.

The best rattling time is a still, crisp dawn. Select a stand where you can see out well but keep hidden. I try to pick a spot where I can sit, and have a tough bush within reach and also a rough-barked tree of fair size like a live oak, plus a patch of gravel or small rocks.   I begin by bringing the antlers smartly together, tines intermeshing, followed with a sharp crack produced by rattling them loudly together.   Then another rattle, and follow up by raking and whacking the dry bush, then raking the points of one antler down the tree bark and finally scraping the points in gravel.   Then one more rattle.   The entire effect sounds like two bucks fighting, breaking twigs, raking trees, and sliding in rock or gravel.

After a brief pause, go through it again or vary it.   Some bucks come on the run, ready to fight.   Some sneak in as if hoping to run off with a doe that is watching two bucks fight.   Young bucks act ridiculously naive at times.   Watch a spike buck and if he turns and stares away from you, look where he looks.   Probably a big buck is coming and the spike isn't anxious to tangle with him.   If you've had no action after you've been on a stand for 20 to 30 minutes, the next tactic is usually to move on.   However, if the place looks good, don't hesitate to stay longer.

One time I began rattling well after dawn, and perhaps 10 minutes later I saw a buck get up from his bed on a nearby ridge.   I was trying to get a buck in for a hunter who was with me.   I kept on, sometimes just raking gravel a little or tickling the antlers lightly.   We were hidden in a small draw and every few minutes we could glimpse a part of the deer moving a step or two along the ridge.   I fiddled with that deer for a whole hour.   I was just about to leave in disgust when the buck, unable to figure out what was going on, walked down off the ridge and into the open and kept walking slowly and stiffly straight toward us.   I didn't dare let him get too close, as alerted as he was.   At possibly 45 yards my hunter dropped him.

Most Texas deer hunters do very little walking.   One reason is that all but a negligible part of the hunting is on private ranch lands, and these have rough vehicle trails gridding them.   Some hunters simply cruise around looking for deer, glassing, making a stalk when possible.   The majority take a stand, either the high variety or on the ground.   Stock-watering "tanks" (ponds) are numerous.   Stands near these are invariably productive, and so are stands on ridges overlooking fairly open valleys.   In some areas, winter wheat and oat patches draw deer by the dozens and are staked out by hunters.

The southern Brush Country gets virtually no walking hunters.   There are sound reasons.   A hunter can jump deer by gingerly prowling the thornbrush but he will seldom get a shot.   Even if he gets a running shot, in such cover they are not very effective and when he wounds a deer in this cover it is too often lost.   Hunting in the Brush Country, when not from a tower, is all stand-hunting of one kind or another.   This region has been sliced up with numerous bulldozed trails, many of them made originally by oil-exploration crews operating seismographs.   These, of course, form open strips through the dense cover.   A perfect stand on such trails is at

Byron Dalrymple brings in a Carmen Mountains whitetail buck. Hunting can be hot and rigorous in the Southwestern deserts. A sportsman should be dressed appropriately and in good physical condition. As in muley hunting in many regions, a good binocular is an extremely valuable piece of equipment.

an intersection that permits you to sit at trailside and watch in four directions by a little slow neck-craning. Another good one in rolling portions of this region is beside a trail at the top of a ridge, so you can see the small valleys on either side.

In moving, deer must cross these trails. Does may dally in them. Bucks seldom do. I've watched a trail intently for hours, then seen a buck barely poke his head and neck out.   That's the time to shoot, if you have any target.   When he crosses it'll be—zip—and that's all.

By preseason scouting on leases or other large tracts, hunters occasionally get big bucks located.   For example, I hunted for seven seasons on a lease of 9,000 acres near Laredo.   The leaseowner was on the property every few days, bass-fishing the several tanks on it.   Thus he knew pretty well the general areas where the most deer were.   When the season opened we took stands, most of the time just below the brow of a hill so we could watch a small valley where good bucks had been seen.   By being above them we could see well down into the dense cover.   Hunting, no matter how you do it in the Brush Country, is difficult; it's challenging because you know there are real trophy whitetails somewhere in the tangle.

In eastern Oklahoma there is much forest land, and hunting methods are just about the same as anywhere east of the Mississippi.   Some hunters love to prowl the woods, some select a stand and stay with it.   I own a small ranch in the Hill Country of Texas that is exceptionally rugged and scenic.   My boys and I have still-hunted the ridges and the brushy canyons there many times, moving very slowly and trying to come up on bucks unaware.   This, too, is interesting hunting because it is difficult.   The same basic technique is used by most hunters in New Mexico and Arizona after Coues deer.   They glass a lot, and pussyfoot around the slopes and the canyons.   They also throw rocks.   That may sound silly, but sometimes it works.   The Coues is a wily little character, and a buck often lies tight and absolutely will not move unless you all but step on him.   Pitching rocks into draws often gets them out.

John Finegan, owner of Dolan Creek Ranch, makes a regular routine of hurling rocks with a big leather sling.   His country is awesomely rugged, with large canyons.   Hurling a few rocks from a rim to go clattering down the canyon soon moves deer.   The only problem with the technique is that it produces running shots.

If I were a nonresident planning to visit the Southwest, I'd first select the state by success ratio and what deer I wanted.   Texas is far and away highest in success.   As I have said, a visitor taking a package hunt has a 100 percent expectation, unless he is trophy hunting.   If I were after Coues deer, although southwestern New Mexico is rather neglected and has a good number, I'd go to southeastern Arizona.   The record book tells why.   Of heads listed in the latest edition, 106 came from Arizona and only two from New Mexico.

To fill yourself in on public lands, the best way in both Arizona and New Mexico is to obtain Forest Service maps showing the national forests.   But for Coues, by all means hire a guide if possible.   Both state game departments may furnish a list (although, of course, no recommendations). In Oklahoma it is possible to get from the game department a listing of state and federal public lands. Many of the state tracts are called public hunting areas. A Forest Service map showing the grasslands and the Ouachita National Forest also would help.

Because the system in Texas is as it is, you won't get far by writing to the game department with a lot of questions. The department keeps no lease lists, day-hunt lists, or package-hunt lists. A Forest Service map will show you the national forests and national grasslands, but these areas won't offer you the best hunting. The route for a visitor is the package hunt. As I mentioned, chambers of commerce are often able to point you toward ranches that offer these. Also, watch the outdoor magazines for ads. Prices vary widely, from a base nowadays of around $150 through a mid-range of about $225 and on up to $400 and $500.

So far as hunting permission is concerned, in New Mexico and Arizona you don't need to worry much since there are ample public lands. In Texas, unless you're a real smooth talker with faith to spare, don't waste valuable time trying to get free access. Deer are a paying crop here. In Oklahoma there are enough public spots, and some private landowners may succumb to a request.

What rifle do you need for the Southwest? I happen to be of the school that thinks it is pure malarkey to believe one caliber is suitable only in the East and another in the West. Certainly some do better than others. By and large, the same calibers are used in the Southwest that are used elsewhere. There are years when it's legal to take four Texas whitetails in a season, and I've done that several years in a row using a .243 with a 100-grain load. I've shot numerous Southwestern deer with the .308. The .30/06, the .270, and comparable calibers are much used. I personally wouldn't hunt without a scope, and my favorite is a 3×–9× variable of top quality. I use one in the live oak and cedar of the Hill Country, and down in the brush, and out in the western mountains for the small whitetails.

Having lived in Texas for almost two decades now, and having hunted the other states under discussion here as well as from Maine to the Great Lakes to the Deep South, it seems to me that some of the most intriguing whitetail hunting on the continent is located here. For example, every deer hunter should eventually make a try for a good Coues buck. This is one of the wariest and smartest of the whitetail tribe. The diminutive Carmen Mountains deer is equally challenging, but not many hunters can get an opportunity to try for it. The first one I took, a young forkhorn, weighed just 45 pounds field-dressed. The last one was an adult, an eight-pointer, and he weighed 76 pounds field-dressed.

As hunter numbers grow and competition for leases in Texas becomes more severe, I presume hunting the mahogany-horned busters of the

Brush Country—which I consider the most challenging of all whitetail hunting—will not be possible for very many sportsmen. But for those who arrange a fee hunt elsewhere in Texas, the deer are certainly present in abundance. In Oklahoma, where deer were exceedingly scarce some years ago, the herd has been steadily expanding and the hunting steadily growing better. Hunting whitetails of the Southwest is an experience quite different from hunting them in other regions, and for my money it rivals the hunting anywhere.

13

Our Whitetail Subspecies—
Seventeen Variations
on a Theme

by Leonard Lee Rue III

Whitetails are not only more numerous and far more widely distributed than mule deer—they also exhibit a far greater number of variations in their form.   That is, they are split into many subspecies.   True, there are also some differing types of muleys.   A small, pale desert muley of the deep Southwest is not quite the same as the big Rocky Mountain strain. But muleys don't arouse nearly the confusion caused by the variations on the whitetail theme, and the two mule-deer subspecies that differ most from what hunters across the country regard as the norm will be covered in separate chapters, one on the Columbian blacktail and one on the Sitka blacktail.   Therefore I've been asked to contribute a chapter intended to unravel the maze of whitetail types.

I can't say that the information I'm about to offer will help you collect venison in your part of the country (although here and there, where I consider habitat differences significant, I'll mention the kind of pockets likely to hold game).   What this information will do is to give you a better idea of the type and size of deer—and the type and size of antlers, the quality of trophies—you're apt to encounter in a given region.   It will also settle a lot of the traditional deer-camp arguments about which subspecies is really being hunted and how it compares with those in other locales. The true hunter wants to learn all he can about his game, so here is a short course in the scientific (and sometimes not so scientific) classification of whitetails.

The whitetail deer is found in all of the contiguous forty-eight states and in eight provinces of Canada.   The latest figures put the total whitetail population at over 11 million.   The whitetail is a member of the Cervidae family, a group that originated in Asia and migrated to this continent, via the Bering Sea Land Bridge, eons ago.   However, the species is a native of North America, having developed on this continent some 20 million years ago.   There are thirty subspecies of this deer recognized today.

151

The author is pictured with a young New Jersey buck. Theoretically, this race, or subspecies, is classified as the Northern woodland whitetail (*O. v. borealis*) but Rue points out that there is much intergrading of races. And in states like New Jersey, which once imported large numbers of deer from other regions, additional interbreeding has occurred. Geographical characteristics have therefore become blurred in many areas. (Photo: Leonard Lee Rue III)

The classification of all living things is known as taxonomy, a most exacting science but one that is split into two warring camps. The rivals have been called the "lumpers" and the "splitters" and both seem to go overboard in their zeal to prove their point and to discredit that of their opponents. The lumpers are those biologists who want to simplify (and perhaps oversimplify) the divisions and the differences found within a single species. The splitters are those who seize upon the slightest (and perhaps imagined) differences, who magnify the differences, and then do

The classification of whitetail subspecies is complicated by interbreeding and by occasional mutations. The Virginia whitetail (*O. v. virginianus*) pictured here is not a true albino but an almost all-white mutant fawn. Lacking natural camouflage, this particular type of mutant has a less-than-average chance of survival. (Photo: Leonard Lee Rue III)

everything possible to justify their reasoning. Both groups tend to go overboard.

A good example is the overclassification of the grizzly brown bear, *Ursus arctos*. Fully eighty-seven North American subspecies have been classified. One splitter claimed that there were several subspecies of the brown bear just on Kodiak Island, and that they did not even interbreed, but he forgot to tell that to the bears. (By the way, subspecies do frequently interbreed where their ranges overlap.) One lumper wants all of the brown bears, found throughout the world, to be classified as a single subspecies. The grizzly bear is currently being grouped with the brown bears as one and the same. While I tend to lean toward the view of the lumpers, I cannot go along with the idea that the high-country silvertip grizzly is the same bear as the coastal brownie. The skull is one of the main means of subspecies identification and the skulls of grizzlies and brownies are almost identical, but there are other physical differences.

A species is an organism that is genetically linked (*genotypic*) so that its members are sexually compatible, making reproduction possible. Most members of most species are also *phenotypic,* all having similar, visible, external characteristics making them identifiable as such. The physiological characteristics that make such identification possible include size, proportion, dentition, epidermal structures and appendages, etc. (However, I must add that in some species size varies astonishingly from one subspecies to another.)

The divisions within a single species creating the subspecies are based on certain factors that are subject to natural rules or laws. Geographic variations are the best examples, for they have evolved changes in size, color, and other adaptations to light, heat, moisture, regional vegetation, and so on.

Most warm-blooded creatures tend to be larger the farther north or south they range from the equator. An accepted biological rule states that body size, in a geographically variable species, averages larger in the cooler parts of that species' range. The larger a body, the smaller is its relative surface and the more efficiently that surface can be heated. Conversely, the hotter the habitat's temperature, the smaller the body and the larger its relative surface, allowing for greater heat dissipation.

My point in explaining all this up is that today there are seventeen subspecies, or "races," of the whitetail deer in the United States and Canada. (And thirteen additional subspecies occur farther to the south; the distribution map in Appendix 1 of this book shows the range of the species as a whole, and a glance at it will reveal that the whitetail is found all the way down into Central America.)

The original divisions of these subspecies were based on skull characteristics, body size, and geographical locations. The little Key deer of

A typical Virginia whitetail (*O. v. virginianus*) in woods maintained by the Tennessee Valley Authority on the Tennessee–Kentucky border.

A Northern woodland whitetail (*O. v. borealis*), the largest subspecies, being field-dressed in the woods near Huntsville, Ontario. (Photo: Ontario Dept. of Tourism & Information)

Florida, *Odocoileus virginianus clavium,* is the smallest deer in the United States, and no one would have difficulty in identifying this unique whitetail race. The largest whitetail deer on our continent, *O. v. borealis,* is found in the northeastern United States and Canada, and most people could not tell it from any of the other large subspecies.

The deer of my home state of New Jersey is classified as *O. v. borealis,* yet I defy any expert in taxonomy to prove this and I'll tell you why. Around 1890, the whitetail deer in New Jersey had been reduced

A Northwest whitetail (*O. v. ochrourus*) being packed out on a trail through national forest land in California. (Photo: U.S. Forest Service)

to less than 200 individuals. In an effort to save the deer, hunting was prohibited, new and stronger game laws were passed—and they were more strictly enforced. These measures helped, but of equal importance was the importation of hundreds of deer from many different states. Deer were purchased by the State of New Jersey and by many private individuals from Virginia, Maine, Michigan, and Wisconsin. Those from Maine, Michigan, and Wisconsin were of the same subspecies as our original deer, but those from Virginia were not. There are no records of the actual numbers imported, nor how many from what state. The im-

A Columbian whitetail (*O. v. leucurus*) with the velvet just peeled from his antlers—a Pacific Coast race found just above and overlapping the range of the Northwest whitetail.   (Photo: Leonard Lee Rue III)

Editor Bob Elman looking over a Texas whitetail (*O. v. texanus*) taken in the west-central part of that state.

ported deer bred with the remnants of the native deer. Since the original importation, many deer have been transplanted, on many different occasions, to many different locations within the state. Yet the subspecies in New Jersey is still classified as *O. v. borealis*. Within the state there is a tremendous variation in the size of the deer, depending on their habitat and the amount, quality, and types of food available. To further complicate the issue, unless there are marked physical geographic differences dividing the ranges of subspecies, there is usually an overlapping or integrading between them, making identification arbitrary.

In many other areas the divisions between whitetail races are similarly blurred, so any grouping by state or region has to be regarded as a generalization. With that qualification in mind, you can form some idea of which deer you're likely to be hunting in your region by reading the following geographical descriptions covering the seventeen subspecies of the United States and Canada.

1. The Virginia whitetail, *O. v. virginianus,* is the prototype of all of our whitetail deer. Fossil remnants were found in a cave in Virginia and named by the naturalist Constantine Rafinesque in 1832. Its range includes Virginia, West Virginia, Kentucky, Tennessee, North Carolina, South Carolina, Georgia, Alabama, and Mississippi. This is a large deer with fairly heavy antlers. It is hunted in all of the states it inhabits, and each state has a good deer population. It has a widely diversified habitat, ranging from the coastal marshes, swamplands, and pinelands to the "balds" found on the top of the Smoky Mountains. In some of the states, the swamps have such dense vegetation and are so difficult to get through that only the use of dogs makes the hunting of these deer possible.

2. The Northern woodland whitetail, *O. v. borealis,* is generally the largest of all the subspecies. The heaviest recorded weight is one from Michigan that tipped the scales at 425 pounds live-weight. It also has the largest range, being found in Maryland, Delaware, New Jersey, Pennsylvania, Ohio, Indiana, Illinois, Minnesota, Wisconsin, Michigan, New York, Connecticut, Rhode Island, Massachusetts, New Hampshire, Vermont, Maine, and in the Canadian provinces of New Brunswick, Nova Scotia, Quebec, Ontario, and a portion of Manitoba. More whitetails of this subspecies are hunted than any other, with some 541,000 deer being legally taken from this area in 1974. This area has also produced eight of the top twenty-five record whitetail heads listed in the Boone & Crockett Records of Big Game. The world-record head, scoring 202 points, was shot in Funkley, Minnesota, in 1918 by John Breen. The right main beam was 31¼ inches long and the left main beam was 31 inches long. The head had 16 points. The winter coat of some of the deer of this subspecies is the darkest of any of our deer.

The range is expanding steadily northward. As the virgin spruce forests of Quebec and Ontario are being cut off for paper pulp, the land is sprouting back with all types of second-growth bushes and trees, producing almost unlimited browse. The wolves that were common in the virgin forest have been pushed back by man's activities in the area. With increased food and decreased predation, this whitetail is expanding both its range and its numbers.

3. The Dakota whitetail, *O. v. dacotensis,* is also a very large deer, run-

A Carmen Mountains doe and buck (*O. v. carminis*) photographed above the Rio Grande near the boundary of Big Bend National Park. (Photo: Leonard Lee Rue III)

A Kansas whitetail doe (*O. v. macrourus*) found by the author grazing amid Oklahoma grasslands. (Photo: Leonard Lee Rue III)

ning about as heavy as the *borealis* in general body weight. When it comes to trophy heads, this subspecies has produced eleven of the top twenty-five records. The range covers North Dakota, South Dakota, and parts of Nebraska, Kansas, Wyoming, Montana, and the Canadian provinces of Manitoba, Saskatchewan, and Alberta. In winter, this deer appears quite dark. The bucks have heavy, fairly widespread antlers.

This is a deer of the riverbreaks. The timbered coulees, gullies, draws, and valleys are its home.

4. The Northwest whitetail, *O. v. ochrourus,* is another large

A Florida whitetail (*O. v. seminolus*) in a Georgia clearing where palmetto thickets can be as lacerating as the mesquite-and-prickly-pear cover of the Carmen Mountains deer.   (Photo: Leonard Lee Rue III)

one.   This deer is found in parts of Montana, Idaho, Washington, Oregon, California, Nevada, Utah, British Columbia, and Alberta.   The largest whitetail I ever saw was either of this subspecies or it could have been a Dakota.   It was in Glacier National Park that I saw this huge whitetail, and the two subspecies intergrade where their ranges overlap.   Not even the experts can agree on exactly where the range of one stops and the other begins.

Although there are no Northwest whitetails in the top twenty-five heads, this subspecies does have very wide-spreading antlers. In coloration, its winter coat is a relatively light cinnamon brown.

5. The range of the Columbian whitetail, *O. v. leucurus,* has been greatly reduced. It formerly ranged along the Pacific Coast in Washington and Oregon, spreading eastward until it intergraded with the Northwest whitetail. Oregon currently does not even give figures for the state population and allows no hunting of them. Washington has a reported 300 to 500 and allows no hunting of them. This subspecies is on the endangered-animal list. It's a large deer with high but narrow-spreading antlers, having no representation in the top twenty-five heads.

6. The Coues, or Arizona, whitetail, *O. v. couesi,* is a small deer. At one time it was thought to be a distinct species but more recent research has relegated it to a subspecies of the whitetail. Although small in general size, it has very large ears, giving it the appearance of a mule deer. It also has a very large tail, leading to its nickname of "fantail." This deer is found in the dry, desert regions of southeastern California, southern Arizona, southwestern New Mexico, and on down into Mexico. (Desert habitat accounts for the oversized ears.) The fantail is apparently isolated from intergrading with the Texas whitetail but it probably does intergrade in the southern part of its range with several Mexican subspecies. Arizona estimates it has about 25,000 Coues deer but does not give any harvest figures. New Mexico has a hunting season for this deer but gives neither a population estimate nor the hunters' take.

7. The Texas whitetail, *O. v. texanus,* is found in western Texas, Oklahoma, Kansas, southeastern Colorado, eastern New Mexico, and the northern portion of Mexico. Everything about Texas is big, even its population of whitetail deer; it has an estimated 3½ million of them. The annual harvest usually goes over 350,000. Texas has four subspecies but the greatest numbers are of the Texas whitetail. The body size of this subspecies is the largest of the Southern forms. The antlers are slender, widespreading, and there are two record heads among the top twenty-five.

8. The Carmen Mountains whitetail, *O. v. carminis,* is a small deer found in the Big Bend region of Texas. The range is limited to just the Carmen Mountains on both sides of the Rio Grande. Not many of these deer are hunted because most of their range falls within the boundaries of Big Bend National Park, where hunting is prohibited. There apparently is no intergrading with the much larger Texas whitetail. A buffer strip of semi-desert and mule deer separates the ranges of the two subspecies.

9. The range of the Avery Island whitetail, *O. v. mcilhennyi,* stretches along the Gulf Coast of Texas and Louisiana. This is the deer of Texas' Big Thicket. It is a large deer, with a dark, brownish winter coat, and it intergrades on the west, north, and east with the whitetails found there.

It is smaller than the Texas whitetail, with antlers that tend to curve sharply inward at the points.

10. The Kansas whitetail, *O. v. macrourus,* is the fourth subspecies occurring in Texas. This deer is found in eastern Texas, Oklahoma, Kansas, Nebraska, Iowa, Missouri, Arkansas, and Louisiana. It is a large deer with very heavy main beams and short tines. Three deer of this type are in the top twenty-five record heads.

11. The Bull's Island whitetail, *O. v. taurinsulae,* is an isolated and very limited race, found only on Bull's Island, South Carolina.

12. The Hunting Island whitetail, *O. v. venatorius,* is another of South Carolina's minor variations, found only on Hunting Island.

13. The Hilton Head Island whitetail, *O. v. hiltonensis,* is still another South Carolinian variation, limited to Hilton Head Island.

14. The Blackbeard Island whitetail, *O. v. nigribarbis,* is found on both Blackbeard and Sapelo Islands of Georgia, and nowhere else.

All of those last four subspecies are medium-size deer with fairly small antlers that are heavily ridged or wrinkled at the base. The islands they inhabit are far enough out in the ocean to prevent intergrading with the subspecies on the mainland or with one another. So far as I can find, hunting is allowed on some, if not all, of these islands.

15. The Florida whitetail, *O. v. seminolus,* is a large deer sporting a good rack. Some of these deer that I photographed in Okefenokee Swamp in Georgia were as large as the New Jersey deer, and some had antlers as large but perhaps not as widespreading. This is the deer of the Everglades.

16. The Florida coastal whitetail, *O. v. osceola,* is found in the Florida panhandle, southern Alabama, and Mississippi. It is not as large as the Florida or the Virginia whitetail but it does intergrade with both.

17. The smallest of the native deer is the diminutive Florida Key whitetail, *O. v. clavium.* The adult buck Key deer stands about 24 to 26 inches high at the shoulder and weighs between 45 and 65 pounds. No hunting is allowed for this race as it is still on the endangered-animal list. In the past, a combination of man's development of the islands, destroying the deer's habitat, plus fires, hurricanes, and lack of hunting control reduced the Key deer population by 1949 to thirty individuals. With better protection and the establishment of the Key Deer National Wildlife Refuge in 1953, this deer's population has been brought back up to about 300. Some of these deer are killed each year by automobiles on the highway that runs through the Keys. If the government would, or could, purchase more land on the Keys before the habitat is destroyed, this deer's future would be assured.

Deer are very adaptable creatures. Many types of wildlife could not withstand the onslaught of civilization; the deer have thrived on it. The

A Florida coastal whitetail (*O. v. osceola*) in the state's panhandle, where this race intergrades with the other Florida subspecies as well as with the Virginia whitetails of Alabama and Georgia. (Photo: Florida Game & Fresh Water Fish Commission)

whitetail deer is the number one big-game animal in the country, and when most people think of deer hunting they think of whitetails. The opening up of the virgin forests, the reduction of the native predators, the planting of new foods that the deer could eat, and proper research, management, and law enforcement have all combined to skyrocket the whitetail population to all-time highs. In some local areas, the deer population will have to decline in the future as man continues to need more land for his own burgeoning population. However, the same factors that increased the deer population should maintain it at the highest levels possible for all time. The future of the whitetail is bright indeed.

PART III

Mule Deer/Blacktails

14

Mule Deer of the Desert

by Sam Fadala

The school bus grumbled to a stop, a cloud of dust from the dirt road boiling up over the back of the vehicle.   The bus constituted a tour.   The teachers and new principal of the desert community's school district were riding the back roads as a familiarization of the students' home area.   I was one of the teachers, and seated next to me was the high school's new principal.   Something I said to the man had caused the bus to be brought to a stop.

All I had said was, "I'll bet there are some nice mule-deer bucks hanging out in those shady sand washes."   The statement was innocent enough, but the principal laughed.

"Sure, right out in that cactus patch, Sam," he chuckled.   "And out there in the brush I suppose there are a few herds of jackalopes running, too, right?"

I retorted that there was no joke to it.   I knew there were some big muley bucks right there in the dry flatlands.   In fact, I was so sure we could find abundant evidence of deer that I bet the man I could turn up good sign in less than five minutes.

"Would you be convinced if I showed you a big track, maybe some droppings, too?" I asked.   He leaned up to the driver and ordered him to stop the bus.

This patch of terrain was in Arizona, not too far from the Mexico border—brushy, sandy, dry.   Once in a while the tall "tree" of the desert, the saguaro, appeared, its arms stretched upward as if in supplication.   And there was the sometimes annoying *cholla,* too, also known as jumping cactus.   Had we looked closely, we might have found delicate greens growing on the desert floor, little filaree, appearing as emerald blades of grass flattened against the ground.

Long, sandy washes crisscrossed the desert floor like creases on the face of an ancient Navajo.   Patches of creosote bush dotted the landscape.   Typical of desert areas, life here would not be readily seen in midday. But almost as if to help me prove my points about the desert, a jackrabbit skittered away in a zigzag course when the man and I stepped out of the bus, and a sentry quail greeted us with its plaintive *che-qui-ta*.

And sure as taxes, there on the ground, pressed into the soft damp sand of a wash, was a track, the telltale points of cloven hooves, large and deep, impressive and proving. The man did not say a word. He looked around at the parched ground, the many kinds of cacti, the cuts of dry washes that could fill with monsoon rains and flood their banks, and the many, many thorny green things that adorned the desert like untouchable vegetable jewelry.

I knew the tracks would be there. Though not seen readily and not hunted to any great degree, the big-eared deer are indigenous to that type of terrain. Depending on where a man has hunted, he may think of mule deer as creatures of the Rockies or perhaps the grasslands and grain fields of the Midwest or—if he has in mind the blacktail variety of muley—the forests of the upper Pacific Coast. But plenty of mule deer flourish in the deserts, too. Not only in this part of the Southwest but in many other desert places, these deer thrive. They may be found on high, cold deserts in Wyoming, or the flatlands of Oregon. Nevada's desert houses them, too, as does the deserts of Colorado, Utah, and Texas. They also range the deserts of New Mexico, Arizona, and Mexico, and even the dry areas in Canada's Alberta and Saskatchewan provinces.

In places men have changed the desert into green fields of crops and the deer change with the terrain, enjoying their own part of the harvest. But they live, too, where it seldom rains and they have adapted to gaining their moisture from plant life, while retaining body fluids by staying out of the hot sun, inactive, brushed up along shady washes and in dark thickets. The most intriguing desert deer I have ever seen were right on the ocean's edge in Mexico's Baja California. Here the big-antlered bucks may come down to the beach at night to pick up seaweed. By day they live in the rugged cactus country, some of the barest terrain I have ever seen.

Given, then, that these deer are present in the desert, often within easy driving distance of hunters, and that they are big deer, sleek, good to harvest for the larder, then why aren't more hunters after them?

Part of the answer was quite clear in the reactions of that high school principal. The man had lived in the Northwest, had hunted his deer in tall pines or brushy wet canyons. He could scarcely believe that mule deer did, indeed, live on the desert. Also, the deer have had a poor press. Commonly, they are thought to be smaller and punier than their mountain cousins. And since they are not easily seen, they have been considered in short supply.

First, the desert deer is not a puny runt. On the average, the animal is

Here's a desert muley of the Southwest in typical cactus, brush, and thornbush country. Desert mule deer are by no means restricted to the Southwest, however. They're also found in the Great Basin and in other arid or semiarid regions—and where they can reach adequate browse and water they often rival Rocky Mountain mule deer as trophies. (Photo: James Tallon)

about the same size as its Rocky Mountain counterpart. I recall a Yuma, Arizona, big-buck contest in which most of the entries were from the famous Kaibab, including a couple of brutes that dressed at over 200 pounds. Yet the winner turned out to be a buck from the desert, and not just any desert but the extremely dry and sterile-appearing Sahara-type terrain around Yuma. That magnificent animal weighed over 225 pounds clean-dressed and his rack, four points to a side, was heavy and wide.

About the only difference between that desert deer and the mountain bucks was color. Mountain bucks tend to be a rich brown while this desert specimen was light gray. This was not an age difference. The deer of the desert areas in the Southwest seem to be lighter in color, closer to gray than to brown.

Now for the second point. I believe that the desert deer are, in some places at least, as abundant per square mile as the mountain deer. In fact, in some forested mountain areas where the trees have denied the forest floor sunlight, food for deer is often less prevalent than in certain desert locales—depending, of course, on rainfall in the desert. No rain, less food. The desert has a remarkable preserving ability for seed, however, and given any moisture these dormant seeds spring to life. In a rainy season in the Southwest recently, scientists were amazed to discover the growth of plants that had not been recorded in the area for 20 years. The seed was there all that time, at rest, waiting for the type of deep-penetrating moisture that would urge growth. Given moisture, then, food is there for the desert deer.

But why bother with desert muleys when there are fine bucks in the mountains? Well, on an autumn day I might opt for the mountains, too, I suppose. But in the dead of winter, I think I would just as soon be on the desert. There are advantages.

First, obviously, there is the good weather of a desert winter in the Southwest. While skies may be overcast and the atmosphere cold in the northern wastelands, and while snow may hamper travel in the mountains, the dryer low places can be most inviting. And there is often a big bonus by way of small-game hunting. A man camped in the desert, say in Arizona in December (and there are special mule-deer seasons at that time in that state as well as an archery deer season) can not only hunt his mule deer, but will also be allowed quail and cottontail, doves at certain times, and waterfowl.

Let's suppose our new arrival to the desert has with him a couple of canteens for water; he is wearing a large comfortable hat to keep the sun off his head and out of his eyes so he can look for deer; he is shod in light birdhunter boots, and he is all ready to harvest some of that desert venison. But after finding tracks just about everywhere, he still hasn't caught sight of a single patch of buckskin. How come? Just what is this desert mule deer all about?

Are these bucks craftier than their high-country cousins? No, not really. No one holds greater esteem for the big desert bucks than I, but the hunter who figures he is being outsmarted by them is shortchanging himself badly. As for cunning, I still have to allow the whitetail, especially the little Coues whitetail buck, an edge over the muley. This is based upon experience with both. These deer don't outsmart us. They outinstinct us. And it isn't so much what they do, but rather what they don't do. They don't move around a lot and they don't stand out like sore thumbs. That light-colored buck dressed in gray is a neutral blend that would darn near outcamouflage camouflage. Put him in a sand wash in the shade and he all but disappears. And he won't be out gamboling about the hills all day. In fact, as with most desert-dwellers, he will feed off and on in the night, eating into early morning, brush up in the shade for most of the day and feed, perhaps heavily, late in the afternoon.

The hunter who knows this will be up early. And he won't be back in camp eating his dinner until after dark. In fact, carrying a flashlight is imperative for the dedicated desert hunter. He should be close enough to camp to make it in without getting lost, but the best place for the hunter to be at dusk is out in the hills looking for deer.

There are several methods of harvesting the desert buck, and each hunter will have to decide his most successful and enjoyable method for himself. But a few basic approaches can be discussed. The simplest, and perhaps not too terribly successful, is the "walk-the-washes" plan. Unfortunately, this means of locating the deer of the desert seems to be most popular. It constitutes a rambling about in a rather aimless way along the washes in hopes of jumping a buck from his bed.

The hunter goes along the edges of the washes, shuffling by each brush pocket that might contain a resting deer, sometimes tossing rocks into these places. Of course, now and then luck will bring the hunter right to the spot and that big buck will jump up, ascend the side of the wash, and perhaps stop long enough to make a sure target of himself.

Another popular method is walking the deer trails and hoping to come upon a feeding buck in early morning or late evening. This means of collecting venison is also chancy. Deer trails in the desert do not seem to be as firmly established as they are in some other habitats, though deer and cattle will often use the same path to a waterhole daily, the cattle drinking at will, the deer waiting until dark or nearly dark.

Waiting in ambush along these trails is particularly fruitless, or has been so far as I have been concerned. Again, these deer are not inclined to move that much, and they do not have to cover huge tracts of land between bedding and feeding grounds. Further, as suggested above, they are most likely to avail themselves of water under the cover of darkness.

Walking with a partner can be an improvement on the walk-'em-out method. One way to use this form of hunter cooperation is to have one

A Southwestern hunter heads for a stand where mule deer often pass close. In desert country, camouflage can be at least as important as in lusher regions unless you're watching for muleys from a high point where the game isn't likely to spot you. Land of this sort may look too barren to support many deer but, as the author points out, the game population per square mile is sometimes higher than in the woodlands. (Photo: James Tallon)

fellow move quickly and quietly along the edge of a wash for maybe 300 to 500 yards. The man who has moved ahead then takes a stand and waits while his partner slowly works up the wash. It helps if the man in the wash has the wind at his back, allowing his scent to go up the wash ahead of him. I have seen bucks catch this scent and move along the belly of the wash. In that event the deer will work right into the partner who has secreted himself up-wash. And if the wind is coming in the direction of the buck and partner in the wash, then the man in ambush has the same wind in his face. If he doesn't move, the buck will not detect him and an easy shot could be the reward.

Some men hunt the desert on the back of a horse or mule. I have never enjoyed desert hunting this way, even though I have found it an interesting way of hunting in the mountains. The desert horseman essentially uses the same tactics as the hunter who walks at random in hopes of scaring something up. Of course, the rider has the advantage of being able to cover many times more territory than the person on foot. He also has the disadvantage of being on the back of an animal, and it's likely that a big buck will let that horse come right past him and not stir from his hidden bed in the shade, preferring to simply sit tight until man and horse have gone away.

A step upward in productivity is the vantage-point, binocular approach. Here our hunter locates a perch that will show him as much terrain as possible. Even on the flatlands there are high points, hills and rock formations, that will put a man above the plain. From these the man glasses. But there is more to this than simply peering in hopes of spotting a buck cavorting about the land.

First, the glass-user must get steady. An unsteady glass will do little good. It only tires the hunter's eyes and can even give him a headache or make him dizzy. Sometimes I use a walking staff on the desert to help me get around. However, since this type of terrain is generally easy to negotiate, the staff is employed more often as a tool for glassing, and it is used in two ways. If I am trying to cover ground between glassing outcrops, I will simply stand and prop the binocular on the padded top of the stick. The stick is made from the stalk of the agave cactus. It is light as balsa and oak-strong. With a rubber crutch bumper on the bottom to quiet its movement, plus a handle of deer hide, tanned and glued in place, and a nice soft top of foam rubber under more tanned hide, it is a highly useful outdoor tool.

If I am seated, I try to locate a good rock to support my back. Then I thrust the stick out in front—jammed into the ground or against another rock. I place the binocular on the padded top of the stick again. There is no heartbeat in that stick to shake the picture. Rested there solidly, I can carefully glass in comfort.

But I do not look for a deer. Because of camouflage, I try to uncover these deer by seeing parts of them rather than whole deer. The rump patch, though somewhat less pronounced than that of the mountain mule deer, is still a telltale sign. So are the light-colored fringes on the ears. Sometimes an eye will glitter. Less often, I have found a rack swaying up above the grasses and brush of a sand wash.

Of course, a combination of methods and a refinement of the hunter's favorite ways are best.   For me, this means plenty of glassing, and I do not mean with the opera-type miniatures that are better suited to a ball game.   I mean with high-quality full-size glasses such as 9×35 binocular or 9×36 or even 10×50.   Such glasses are great aids in deerfinding.   Remember that the object is to try to find a camouflaged creature.   This means definition, which is that quality in optics that allows the hunter to discern between the dead branch of a fallen tree and the bony curve of a big buck's rack.   To define—that is what definition is all about, and it comes with top-quality glasses.

Between sessions of glassing, and while walking from one point to another, I try to remain alert and I wouldn't think of passing a brush pile without giving it a kick or tossing a rock in on the chance that a big buck might be taking his siesta in there.   If I'm with a friend, we might team up and try to work the washes so that one of us might chase a buck to the other guy.   And when I feel very ambitious I will even glass the sides of hills for bedded deer, as the big muleys will sometimes rest on these open hillsides on pleasant winter days.

Where to glass?   When I look out across the terrain I try to pick out places that appear to have the low browse type of plants so loved by the big bucks.   In early morning and late afternoon my glass has often picked out the feeding deer.   Without camouflage, these bucks would be actually quite easy to find as they will often feed right out in the open.   But they blend well, and even though there may be but a few low bushes the animals can still be very hard to detect.   It takes patience.

Outfitted with canteens for water, stout pants that will ward off the catclaw thorns, light boots, and a decent hat, plus that pair of good binoculars and maybe the walking stick, the hunter is ready to go after the deer of the desert.   By combining several methods and by using those glasses, he begins to weave a pattern of success.   There are desert hunters who come home year after year with their venison because they have worked up a method that is right for them.   But how do they find the hot spots, those places that house the big boys?

Scouting is the way.   By scouting, I mean looking for those bucks after first getting a lead from fellow hunters, ranchers, game officials, and any other source, using topo maps, and working out the country to find the deer before the season.   Many a Sunday picnic has turned out to be a scouting trip when the man who is driving the family for a sunny visit to the outdoors comes across a likely place for desert deer.   He checks for sign, then he comes back with topo map in hand and he looks the country over carefully.   He may well have a place that will render a good harvest come season.

As for a choice of arms, there is plenty of cracker-barrel philosophy to apply here and there is always the fun of argument when caliber choice is brought up, be it for Tanzania elephant or Ohio groundhogs.

Ironically, the basic problem is that there is no problem. We have so many good mule-deer calibers suitable for desert hunting that the choice is sometimes difficult, though it should not be. The best way to make your selection is to match the rifle or pistol to your circumstances and technique.

The standard—and excellent—guns and cartridges are discussed elsewhere in this book, and most readers will be happy with one or another of the recommendations. But some of us do have special problems or desires. I have a friend who harvests his desert venison as an incidental bonus while hunting Gambel's quail. He carries a drilling—one of those triple-barreled European creations featuring side-by-side smoothbores

Out in the wide open spaces of the Western deserts, shots at mule deer can be as long as in Eastern chuck hunting. This hunter has stationed himself on a point overlooking a wide valley through which seasonally migrating muleys pass. He's using a .25/06 target rifle mounted with a 4× Weaver scope. (Photo: Norm Nelson)

On the desert as in the woods, the two-man drag is frequently the only practical way to get a deer back to your hunting car. If you're lucky, though, the dragging distance may be shorter in the flatter parts of arid country because there's no big timber to stop a 4WD. (Photo: Russell Tinsley)

plus a rifled barrel. His model combines the 12-gauge with a 7×57mm rifle. Another acquaintance is a backpacker who shaves every possible ounce from the weight of his gear. His personal solution was a rifle made by Frank Wells of Tucson, a custom specialist who hand-built him a 6mm/222 that feels like a powder puff when compared to some of the blunderbusses I've toted. With hot handloads, it fires an 80-grain bullet at about 2,950 fps. Is that enough for mule deer? Well, it develops energy about like the factory-loaded .250 Savage cartridge. This means it's effective at limited distances, though I've seen it perform impressively on game. I'd say it's a 150-yard killer for the hunter who stalks his deer and shoots accurately.

Another solution for the man who wants to go light is—obviously—a handgun. Those of you who would prefer something really small— something that rides in a holster—should read Chapter 6 on side-arm hunting for deer, and give Steve Ferber's suggestions very serious consideration. Also becoming more popular, not just on the deserts but everywhere, is the muzzleloader. And those of you who want to try black powder should read Chapter 7 by Bill Hughes. Incidentally, while I haven't yet taken a mule deer with my Numrich .58 modified underhammer, I have killed other game with it and I wouldn't hesitate to take after the biggest mule deer in the land with a properly loaded muzzle gun.

And then there is archery. The mule-deer hunter who has selected the bow as his tool would be well advised to use the high-hill, glassing technique. Then the game will be spotted before it spots the hunter and a good stalk can be made. Waiting at waterholes can sometimes produce good shooting, too, but as mentioned above, the bucks may not come to drink until after shooting hours.

As this is being written, I have been in preparation for a desert muledeer hunt with the bow. Deciding that archery was going to be added to my means and methods of filling the freezer, I went all out and began hunting small game and found that with my compound bow I could raise a lot of the devil with game up to 50 yards. Considering that a 50-yard distance is quite possible to attain in the desert when the game is spotted first, I am confident that I will feed the family with my Robin Hood forays. I learned that a good set of matched arrows was a must and I rigged my bow with a cushion plunger, a device that stabilizes my arrow flight, and a hunting stabilizer to dampen the vibration of the outfit. I use a bowsight with four pins, and my arrows seem to find the mark every time if I do my part, sighted-in for 20, 30, 40, and 50 yards.

Desert mule-deer hunting will be around as long as man refrains from covering the desert with concrete and exercises some common sense in game management. Despite what seems at first glance to be the world's most hostile terrain, the desert does quite well in feeding and taking care

The rack on this muley won't make the record book, but you can tell at a glance that he's a buck worth taking—well nourished by browse that may appear inadequate to a hunter who isn't familiar with desert habitat. (Photo: Norm Nelson)

of its own. If anything, it is a shame that more good venison is not brought to the pan by means of a swift harvest by either well-placed rifle or pistol shot or razor-sharp arrow.

Natural enemies of the mule deer on the desert are few (unless one includes occasional prolonged drought among natural enemies). However, coyotes do eat fawns. Contrary to the current TV campaign, with ads written by desk-bound city dwellers who are not even remotely versed in science, the coyote does not live on discarded peanut-butter sandwiches and crumpets alone. As my family has witnessed, they will ambush deer at waterholes and kill them. This is not an indictment of coyotes but it is a call to deal with them rationally, where possible and necessary, through management (not eradication). A fawn crop in the desert will be thinned by the little howlers, and since hunter success is usually low on the desert, this can be good—certainly better than having the deer destroy their own range should their numbers mount too high for the habitat. Where hunters are using deer for harvest, and where they wish to retain and maintain that population, a modest coyote-control program may be in order.

The feline predators are no problem on the desert. The bobcat has never appeared to be in any great number nor has it caused the decline of deer herds. As for the larger deer eater, the puma, its range is normally in the mountains. Thus, we conclude that by leaving habitat for the desert deer, by hunting to promote a reasonable harvest, and by engaging in a mild coyote-control program when game officials find it wise, we should have mule deer on the desert for a long time.

15

High-Country Hunting in the Rockies

by Norman Strung

Is mule-deer hunting in the northern Rockies all that it's cracked up to be? You bet it is, and more. Taking up the trail of a big muley is excitement enough, but that first step also leads to woodland parks dappled with wildflowers, into tumbledowns of crags and peaks, and through the wildest country in the nation. It's an unbeatable combination: raw beauty and the challenge of a magnificent animal, finely attuned to his environment. But such a dream hunt isn't without a few rude awakenings that you had better open your eyes to before heading west.

Licenses should be your first consideration. Ten years ago, a nonresident could walk into any crossroads general store in Idaho, Montana, or Wyoming, plunk down $20 to $50, and pick up his deer tag. Today, things have tightened up considerably.

Prices for both resident and nonresident licenses have risen astronomically in the Rocky Mountain states. In Montana, for example, a nonresident has to pay $225 for a ''sportsman's license'' that allows him to shoot two deer and an elk. Single-species permits are virtually unavailable.

Over-the-counter sales will also be curtailed. Nonresidents will have to apply directly to the fish and game department to purchase their licenses, and only a limited number of out-of-state licenses will be sold—first come, first served.

Resident hunting patterns in Montana have been similarly altered. At one time it was easy to shoot two mule deer in a season. Now that second deer, if you want it, must be a whitetail. And there are intricate regulations regarding hunting districts, the length of seasons, whether or not you can shoot antlerless deer, a potpourri of laws that would confuse a Philadelphia lawyer. And similar changes are taking place in Wyoming, Colorado, and Idaho—virtually every Western state.

No, I don't like these developments either, but let me point out that all these annoyances are designed to preserve the object of my affection—the quality of hunting in the West.

The big muleys are still present in great number; the clear air still greets you every morning; the mountains haven't changed. What has changed is the kind of hunt you must plan. Gone are the days when four buddies got together on a Tuesday night and casually decided to fly to Idaho for a hunt the next week. Changed, too, is the resident's plan to shoot two deer on a Saturday morning, 15 minutes outside town. Hunting today's West requires planning, and careful attention to detail. Arrange the fundamentals of your trip early. Get license fees in the mail well in advance of deadlines. Study regulations, limits, and area boundaries carefully. In short, know exactly what you're getting into.

With this change in emphasis from casual to careful, time becomes extremely important. You're making a large investment in licenses, perhaps guide fees, and time spent planning. This investment should be at least matched by the time you spend afield.

If you live so far from the Rockies as to make your hunt a one-trip affair, I'd say a week should be the minimum time you budget for your hunt. If you plan several trips, try to set aside at least four hunting days for each visit. Even residents who live close to good hunting are better off if they make their hunt an overnighter. You need the time not just to get into the good hunting country, but to analyze and learn the terrain and the habits of the native deer. Sure, you could stumble across a Christmas tree of a rack your first day out, but there are long odds against it. Dame Chance is a notoriously fickle provider.

Conditioning is another investment you must make if you're going to take your muley hunt seriously. The physical condition (or lack of it) of the clients I guide has proved to be the most important factor contributing to their chance of success. More times than I can count, the stamina required to hike that extra mile, to climb another 300 vertical feet to a rock outcrop, or to sprint uphill for 50 yards to an overlook has meant the difference between success and failure.

A specific example of how conditioning can come into play happened to me several years ago. I was hunting in Montana's Bridger Mountains right after a 6-inch snow had blanketed the area. I was counting on the fresh snow to reveal the elevation where the big bucks were hanging out. I'd climbed steadily for two hours and had topped out on a ridge when I cut my first big track, no more than a half-hour old by the condition of the disturbed snow crystals.

Although tracking down a buck isn't the best way to get a shot, I was interested in learning what this fellow was up to, so I stayed with his prints. Not 300 yards ahead, the straight path he took began to meander;

In the high country of Wyoming, Idaho, Montana, and the other Rocky Mountain muley regions, a hunter can often glass wide expanses from the crests of ridges. But if he spots what he wants, he may then have a long and difficult stalk before he can get within shooting distance.

a sure sign he was looking for a place to lie down, and a good indication that I'd come too far. I quickly looked around and, sure enough, caught a flash of mouse-brown flickering through the timber. I cursed my luck and impetuousness, but decided to play a hunch because the buck was running downhill.

I knew of a small dip in the ridgeback perhaps a quarter-mile away (Westerners call it a saddle) and by the direction that muley was headed, there was a good chance he'd use the saddle for an escape route to higher ground. Heels and snow flew as I struggled to reach the pass before the deer, and the uphill run, a few drifts, and 7,000 feet of elevation just about did me in. But when I got to the saddle there he was, bouncing along with the curious spring-loaded muley gait. I got a solid shooting rest to compensate for my heaving chest and dropped the four-pointer with a spine shot.

Admittedly, outrunning a muley is seldom a successful technique, but there will be many times when comparable stamina will make the difference between meat in the pot and track soup.

What's the best means of conditioning? Jogging builds up your wind. That's half the battle, but you won't be in real shape until you can climb eight flights of stairs without discomfort. And remember, you'll be doing that kind of climbing in the rarified air of 4,000- to 8,000-foot elevations, with approximately 20 extra pounds of rifle, shells, boots, clothing, and sandwiches.

To some extent, this initial advice might read like a good-news bad-news story, but the preceding "bad news" is modern hunting reality. Now the good news. There are more and bigger muleys in the Rocky Mountains than ever before. From the standpoint of numbers and quality of their quarry, Western deer hunters have never had it so good. Each year finds more and more deer in the Rockies. It's a controlled "explosion" brought about by careful management, and the net result is maximum numbers of deer for the available food supply. These large populations are reflected in hunter-success figures. The "average" Western state posts a figure of around 65 percent success. In my native Montana, hunters score about 90 percent of the time, bagging close to 100,000 deer a year.

The success ratios, balanced against the total harvest, are good indicators of the kind of hunting you can expect in a particular area, and I'd suggest you include a review of these figures as part of your preliminary plans. But no matter which state you choose for your hunt, there are some hard-and-fast rules about where you'll find deer in the Rockies.

The most animals will be concentrated in and around the band of forest where timberlands meet fertile bottomlands. The cover will be a mix of conifers and deciduous brush that melt into pasture, farmland, or cottonwood-and-aspen riverbottoms below. It's this type of terrain that affords a muley a mix of choice foods, escape cover, and shelter in the winter.

However, while this kind of country supports the densest populations of deer, *resident* animals will invariably be does, young-of-the year, and forkhorn-to-four-point bucks. These animals make for excellent eating, and a few of those four-pointers carry mount-worthy racks, but the real trophies will be found at much higher elevations.

Fully mature mule-deer bucks are solitary creatures that will tolerate neither the company of their kind nor human incursion. Their superb condition affords them the latitude to migrate yearly between summer and winter ranges—distances that often exceed 50 miles. If a wrist-thick rack is your idea of a hunt, look for these animals in the forests and parks that lie within a mile of timberline. They'll remain in this kind of country until they are driven down by severe storms and deep snow, or the madness of the rut.

It might be worth pointing out something about hunting these trophy-class deer though; it's a demanding sport—demanding in the preparations you must make if you want to organize your own hunt, demanding in terms of cost if you hire a guide, demanding in the sheer energy required of you, and demanding in, for lack of a better word, concentration. When you hunt among the heavy populations of muleys at lower elevations, you're always seeing deer. Sure, the majority of them won't wear horns, but there's always an electric excitement that accompanies a glimpse of any deer, and when you see a dozen a day you're enjoying the hunt even if you never touch the trigger. In the sky-high sanctuary of trophy-class bucks, there are fewer animals per square mile. You hunt harder and see less, and as a result, your interest wanes. Any hunter who lacks a keen edge of anticipation, and the concentration it engenders, is in the woods with two strikes against him. And therein lies the reason why some hunters who specialize in big muleys score every year while many others don't. The "experts" know and satisfy the demands of concentration. They look harder, they hunt longer, they cover more ground, and they harvest the trophy bucks.

OPPOSITE PAGE: Many Easterners think that Rocky Mountain muley hunting is mostly a matter of cruising (by foot, horseback, or vehicle), glassing, and then carefully squeezing off long shots. But some of the best hunting is in brush that looks surprisingly like Eastern whitetail woods—as shown in this photo of a Wyoming muley buck. (Photo: Wyoming Game & Fish Dept.)

This scene is in the Rockies, but it looks a lot like some other parts of the country—including more than one stretch of Maine woods. Still-hunting can pay off in habitat like this, and so can a carefully planned drive.

A hunter (right) and his Montana guide-outfitter inspect the placement of a .264 Magnum bullet that produced a quick one-shot kill. The buck was quartering away, and the bullet traveled forward into the lung-heart area. The guide has his dressing knife out, and the hunter is about to roll the muley into position for evisceration. (Photo: Camera Associates)

Whether you choose to hunt the butter-bucks of lower elevations or the trophy muleys of the high country, the key to taking these deer lies in a thorough understanding of their habits. Muleys move about morning and evening, and this is the time to watch and wait. Find a rocky outcrop or an overlook with an unobstructed view, and use a combination of your naked eyes and a scope or binoculars to scan the terrain. Use your eyes to detect movement, and your optics to identify what you saw move. There's a good chance you'll get a shot from this kind of stand. If you see a deer with your name on it moving toward you, the cardinal rule is avoid being "sky-lighted." Get in back of something, or

The author (right) and one of his successful clients drag out a good buck. Strung emphasizes the need for physical conditioning to withstand the rigors of this kind of hunting.

get something in back of you to break up your outline. Muleys aren't quite as sharp-eyed as whitetails, but they're quick to perceive the outline of a man, and its implications.

There's an even better chance you'll spot a deer that isn't following a path that will take him close to your stand. Mark the route he takes—for here, too, muleys follow certain patterns. They go downhill to feed, they go uphill to bed, and generally they move in a straight line, breaking right or left only when they near the feeding or bedding area. When you see where a deer's headed, you've got a good clue to his future location, and a good chance for a successful stalk.

When stalking muleys, you must go high and come down on the deer. If you try to approach them from below, every protective mechanism at the animal's disposal is working for him and against you. He's still got quite a few tricks going for him when you come down from above, but at least you've canceled some of his life insurance: his habit of facing downhill, his dogged instinct to escape by running uphill, and the messages carried by the winds. In the daytime, breezes normally blow from canyon bottoms to mountaintops.

When working down on a deer it's extremely important to move slowly. Assume each step you take is the one that will reveal some great, bedded buck, and concentrate on seeing him before he sees you. At this point of the hunt, your eyes become your most important asset, for when you see a muley before he sees you, you've got him if you can shoot straight.

In the event that you spook your quarry, you can again depend on most muleys to respond to habit. Their first move will be to run directly away from you, but you can bet your favorite hunting boots that they'll soon cut left or right, then double back uphill, usually sticking to the brush of a coulee or canyon. It's in this situation that a sprint occasionally pays off.

While I can talk about this notion of predictability with honest conviction, I must also point out that as the muley you set your sights on gets bigger, older, and wiser, he becomes less locked into "normal" patterns. In the course of becoming a trophy-class animal, he'll surely have a few brushes with hunters, and will develop some unique traits as a result. The classic example is that last look back. When you spook a young animal, you can whistle, yell, even take a shot in the air, and the critter will stop and look back, usually just before he reaches cover. I've tried that trick or seen it tried on five trophy-class muleys to date, and it had no effect whatever.

Another example of the kind of odd savvy muleys get with age occurred just last year. Eli Spannagel, Carroll Kaup, and I were hunting the sarpy breaks on Eli's huge Montana ranch. The country amounts to rough, brushy drainages that slough off a high plain, and the common hunting technique is to drive a pickup from canyon head to canyon head, then walk out the coulees.

We were heading for our chosen hunting spot, driving along a ranch road, when Eli slowed the pickup to a crawl and looked quizzically into some brush that marked the start of a small coulee.

"That's a funny-looking tree," he said.

Carroll followed the direction of Eli's gaze and screwed up his eyebrows. "That's not a tree, that's a set of horns!"

"No," replied Eli, "horns can't be that big."

At that instant, the tree stood up and was found to be attached to the biggest muley any of us had ever seen.

There was a mad scramble for guns. By the time cases were thrown off and shells jacked into chambers the deer was long gone, but Eli knew his ranch. He roared off, as fast as his short legs could carry him, heading for a point of rocks with a grand view of the country below. It would be a long shot, but that deer had to pass within range. A quarter of an hour later, the three of us had watched from that windy promontory until our eyes teared. We hadn't seen a sign of the super-buck.

"I can't understand it." Eli shook his head. "He had to pass at least within sight."

"Maybe he crawled into a prairie-dog hole," Carroll hypothesized.

It seemed more logical than what actually happened, for when we neared the pickup, Eli once more uttered an epithet of disbelief, raised his .270, and shot the biggest buck of his life. The animal was peering at us from the shade of a huge ponderosa pine not 20 yards from the brush where we'd first spotted him. It's that kind of unpredictable behavior that often makes a big buck so tough to come by—and also makes him such a special prize.

While that buck's reaction was unusual, so was the fact that he was downed at such close range. As a rule, muley hunting is a long-shot proposition. If you're unfamiliar with targets at 200- and 300-yard distances, be sure to make rifle practice part of your preparations. One thing my clients have taught me is to impress this need on anyone who lives east of Minnesota. When otherwise capable hunters are confronted with a 300-yard shot from a prone position, 50 percent of them crumble under the strain, a strain that I might add is totally imagined.

Expect most shots to fall between 100 and 300 yards. While there are exceptions that will occur, that kind of average distance is best handled by calibers in the neighborhood of the .25/06, the .270, and the .30/06. If you get much more powerful than a .30/06, you'll do gross damage to muley meat at 100-yard ranges, and rifles with loads lighter than the .25/06 don't pack the power to kill cleanly beyond 300 yards. I know I'm opening a can of worms with these statements—sure, a well-placed shot from virtually any centerfire rifle will kill a muley at 300 yards—but long experience and many misses have proved these three to be the most able calibers in most situations. My personal favorite is the .270. I consider it *the* caliber for mule deer.

I'm similarly opinionated on the use of scopes. They are nearly as important as your rifle when you're after mule deer. Snap shots at muleys are as rare as elephants in Iowa, so open sights are of no advantage. The precision aiming provided by crosshairs is also welcome on long shots, and you'll use your scope's magnifying ability to examine a hundred things in the course of a day afield. When it comes to magnification, there are excellent arguments for both 2½× and 4×. I have never found a need for a fixed-power scope above 4× when hunting mule deer,

After a productive day's hunt, a mule deer is hung before sunset at Strung's camp. But don't count on collecting venison and a good trophy that fast.

and while variables can be handy I've had several unfortunate experiences when clients forgot to turn back to 3× or 4× after examing a coyote at 10, and completely blew a shot because they couldn't find the animal in the scope. Variables also add extra weight to the package you must lug up and down mountains.

But for all the excellent and carefully chosen equipment at a hunter's disposal, the most powerful ally you'll ever know is savvy, and learning to take racks regularly from the high country is an education that requires many years of careful study. If I had to sum up the differences between hunting the lowland whitetail and the mountain muley, I'd say taking muleys on the Rockies is deer hunting on a grand scale. Distances are greater, the physical and mental demands are greater, but to my way of thinking so are the rewards.

16

Grain-Belt Muleys

by Bert Popowski

The era of the trophy hunter has nearly ended or, at best, is waning due to the sheer cost of guided trips for high-ranking heads to grace spacious trophy rooms. The traditional trophy hunter, who traveled to far-distant lands in a quest for a wide assortment of species, has been replaced by sportsmen of modest means who have turned to hunting for mature specimens of only a few species. If these wear splendid headgear, that's fine. But as a rule the main targets of such hunters are animals of outstanding eating qualities, those that can be served with pride to friends who may never have feasted on any meat that didn't come from a supermarket. One of life's delights for me has been the conversion of prissy people, mostly urbanites, who shrank from tasting the produce of my generous arsenal of firearms.

The flavor of most meat varies enormously according to the factors existing at the time the animals were harvested. It doesn't depend only on whether the critters are skinny or fat, male or female, young or adult. In the final analysis, it depends on the kind of food your game tucked away for weeks before you collected it. Of course, if you're a slob in the postmortem care of your game, you can ruin grand eating through sheer ignorance. But that isn't the game's fault.

In the case of venison, the quality depends on the time of year when your buck was shot, the neatness with which he was dispatched, field-dressed, and cooled out, and, above all, the kind of food on which he had been living. A buck taken late in the rut (or after it) is seldom any great eating prize. I say "seldom" because an over-the-hill buck that had little or no interest in pursuing does frequently produces venison steaks you can cut with a fork. In comparison, a rut-gaunted muley provides stringy and often musky meat.

Similarly, a buck that has been crippled and chased hard until he is finished off provides equally poor venison. Injury or fright will pump adrenalin into his bloodstream and thence throughout his muscular fibers. This toughens the meat and gives it a rank taste.

Even if none of these detrimental factors applies to the buck you bag, there's the possibility that your game lived on foods which embittered his flesh or, in some cases, gave it a bland tastelessness that says nothing for its eating qualities.   Year after year, certain areas produce venison of the highest quality and others don't.

For instance, regardless of deer species, I wouldn't give much for a buck that has been fattened strictly in cornfields, with no nourishing and mild-flavored browse or mast to enrich the venison's flavor.   Corn merely lays on the tallow and does little to give the meat tastiness.   But if a deer feeds on small grains and then has access to such legumes as clover or alfalfa, or hazel or oak browse and mast, then I'll sprain my running gear to put my tag on him.   Such "finishing" foods put a flavor into venison that makes it equal, and sometimes superior, to beef that has been fattened in pens.   Lucky are the hunters who can pursue their venison in such grain-belt areas, for their bucks are tops in taste

There's a big stretch of the Midwest (and that part of the West just beyond it) where the deer are big, the meat excellent, and the muleys populous enough to provide excellent hunting for those who know how, when, and where to collect their venison, and what sort of rifle to rely on for long shots at deer in open country.

For some inexplicable reason, *Odocoileus hemionus* joined many other wild species in being abundant in the western United States but never crossed the Mississippi.   Muleys come in nine "races" or subspecies that range from southwestern Canada throughout the Rockies and into northern Mexico.   The Rocky Mountain form is advertised as the largest but bucks from the Grain Belt of the Midwest are their match.   The easternmost range in any significant quantity begins at the edge of the Corn Belt, where corn and soybeans displace small grains as the major cash crop.   So the muleys of which I write seldom get east of a center line drawn through the twin Dakotas and the same longitude passing through the tier of states to their south.

This is a vast area of open country, large tracts of which have been designated as part of the national grasslands.   During the early 1930s, when the grasslands were abused by overgrazing, the Great Depression and the severe Dust Bowl droughts and dust-drifting winds forced many landowners into bankruptcy.   A great deal of acreage was retired from private ownership and thrown into a pool of land devoted exclusively to holding the soil and grazing a limited number of cattle.

South Dakota, as only one of eleven Western states participating in the National Grasslands Act, has a total of 864,268 acres in three plots in the grasslands program.   It also has some 240,000 acres of public hunting lands administered by its game department.   Much of the grasslands part of this open range is excellent muley range simply because it is lightly

These Montana bucks are typical of the well-fed muleys found in that state and eastward into the Dakotas. The author points out that mule deer are quite gregarious before the onset of the rut—which means that if you see a buck, there are likely to be others in the vicinity. Frequently you'll have to choose between two or more bucks like these. The one to the rear has the better rack. (Photo: E. P. Haddon, U.S. Fish & Wildlife Service)

subjected to human use. All of South Dakota's grasslands are located west of the Missouri River, in an arid, lightly populated area. They form a choice hunting portion of that grain-belt muley range I mentioned.

Muleys differ hugely from whitetails in their appearance, locomotion, and behavior. Hunters acquainted only with the whitetail can do themselves a big favor by studying all they can find about muley habits before taking after these deer of the spacious West. Basically, the difference in performance is this. When jumped, whitetails dodge into the nearest cover, around a ridge point or down into a valley; muleys, even when wounded, usually go up because generations of them have found safety in elevations. If there's no height of land within reasonable reach, a muley will take off across country, substituting miles of distance for a few hundred feet of elevation.

The term "grasslands" doesn't mean that all the easterly mule-deer range consists of flat or gently rolling prairies. There's some rugged terrain on the eastern side of the Rockies. Here Popowski takes a comfortable seat on a high lookout slope commanding a wide view. (Photo: Bert Popowski)

When hunted hard, whitetails learn to hide better on their crowded home range, sometimes concealing themselves in bits of low brush scarcely adequate to hide a cottontail. But muleys, used to spacious country, seldom tolerate much hunting pressure. They just abandon disturbed areas for more isolated spots.

Finally, muleys are very gregarious, though they may be separated by sexes before the rut. Thus, if you see one buck, large or small, you can be almost positive you're close to others and they're probably watching you. When one goes, they all move out. One time, after hunting hard during most of a very windy day without finding a hair of my game, I came up a slight rise into the wind. As my eyes uncovered a small bench it exploded with bucks, nine in all. By the time I had sorted them out and chosen "my" buck, they were all out of sight. I didn't get off a shot.

In open country, such as the comparatively level terrain devoted to raising grain and forage crops, it often pays to lean heavily on binocular prospecting instead of exposing yourself excessively by extensive walking or driving. Any bit of rough country, regardless of its vegetation, should be carefully glassed. Muley bucks may bed in the shade of a lone sagebrush or a single bush on an otherwise barren slope, or behind a tiny wrinkle in the land where vegetation is too short to hide behind. Look for wee flats just large enough to provide bedding space for a deer, or a notch or dry wash that will provide level spots in the shade. An inexperienced hunter can miss dozens of such semi-exposed hideaways because he can't believe good bucks could hide so well. Thousands of muleys have lived long and undisturbed lives because such cover wasn't adequately investigated. A buck with towering antlers may stretch his neck, lay his chin on the ground, and become a part of an enormous drab landscape which surrounds him on every side.

When actually working up on a buck discovered in such open hideouts, a direct foot approach simply allows him to slip away along one of several escape routes. But two hunters working together can move game toward each other, provided one of them ambushes the right escape route and covers it well. And, of course, a good long-range rifleman may be able to nail his trophy by simply spanning a range of several hundred yards.

Two types of acreage often serve as incubators for splendid muley bucks. One is the lavish scattering of historic or commemorative areas set aside as national monuments or parks. A Minnesota friend. who regularly hunts in Montana, usually drives through both ways at night to reduce the traffic he encounters. His favorite route goes past the Theodore Roosevelt National Monument in North Dakota, which serves as a home for some magnificently antlered trophies. At dusk they leave this refuge to feed on surrounding croplands and are often sighted approaching their dining areas. The extensive Badlands National Monument of my home

Popowski (right) and his partner, Don Baldwin, look over a grand mule-deer buck taken on a grassy flat near the Cheyenne River.   (Photo: Bert Popowski)

state of South Dakota is another producer of grand heads; so is Wind Cave, scarcely a dozen miles away from where this is being written.   Wise hunters scout the surrounding areas, determine the travel routes used by their game, and try to intercept them at dusk or dawn.

Then there's the second category of promising acreage: Any prominent feature of the country that's rugged in its topography is bound to attract fine muley bucks.   For instance, such landmarks as buttes and hills are magnets for assorted wildlife, including fine mule deer.   After a week of open season, they won't be exactly in those landmarks but bedded out in such open spots as I've previously described. Such breaks of rough country, though they may be miles away from croplands, provide sanctuary for grain-belt bucks. Mule deer, unlike whitetails, think nothing of sauntering a dozen miles a night to feed.

Just how big are big muleys? Again, unlike whitetails, they don't run off their tallow in nervous jitterings, so they're usually in better flesh than their cousins. When they travel it's usually at a leisurely pace because their routes have been chosen to keep them off skylines and only occasionally crossing thoroughfares of significant local travel. The biggest grain-fed muleys will regularly outweigh equally well-fed whitetails in live weight. Top bucks may dress out at slightly over 300 pounds, indicating a live weight in the close-to-400-pounds range. Whitetails of that size have been recorded but they're much rarer. Even young muley bucks are invariably bigger and heavier than whitetails of similar age.

Archers are exceptionally successful in grain-belt muley hunting because they can waylay their game along established travel routes or in the rougher bits of habitat. I've known of archers meeting their game literally head-on, with shots taken at around 10 yards. In one sharply eroded Badlands formation I once watched an archer and a buck, on opposite sides of a knife-edged ridge, trying to outwait each other while separated by a mere dozen feet. The bowman finally blew it by shuffling his feet and the buck made long tracks. Since archery seasons usually precede firearms seasons, many muleys become quite apprehensive of ambushes. Then they come out later in the dusk hours and get back to safe sanctuaries before dawn breaks on the rifle hunters.

The connoisseur of choice venison will do his deer hunting as early as the opening of the season permits. He will also field-dress his buck as rapidly as possible, protect it against insects, birds, and beasts, and haul it in to some means of controlled cooling and ageing for at least a week at a constant temperature of around 40 degrees. Skinning should be delayed to avoid dehydrating the meat unless the weather is so hot that skinning in the field is mandatory to help get rid of the critter's body heat. If the temperature is right, just a bit above freezing, ageing goes on equally well with pelt on or off.

Since muleys are often killed in out-of-the-way places, some gentle means of getting the field-dressed carcass out to terminal transportation is advisable. If you just knock over your venison, gut it, drain it, and then immediately drag it roughly over rocks, stumps, and other obstacles, you'll bruise the meat. Severely bruised spots will become bloodshot. So the carcass should be bled thoroughly and allowed to cool enough to firm up, stiffening somewhat before being dragged. Even then, choose the smoothest drag route. It's a shame to batter choice meat.

Partly because they don't instantly hit the panic button on discovery, muleys lay on considerably more tallow in preparation for the lean months. This conditioning weight is rapidly shed by the bucks during the rut, indicating the value of making early-season hunts to harvest the best venison. Does do not shed their conditioning tallow during the rut, though they do gradually pay it out during the long months of winter pregnancy. That's why our forefathers used to prefer to take does for winter meat. Though smaller in total weight, they were in better condition than post-rut bucks and so yielded tastier venison.

Another facet of bringing home fine venison is using a rifle that will kill cleanly if the buck is well hit. Although muleys are big deer, outsized cannons aren't needed to knock them down. After all, they're only deer, and a rifle suitable for whitetails will do a good job on muleys at similar distances. The main difference is that most muleys are taken at somewhat longer than usual whitetail distances so the hunter should be prepared—by practice, attitude, and rifle—to take his game at moderate antelope ranges. Which is to say his rifle should be zeroed-in to hit on point-of-aim at 200 yards and he should memorize its trajectory at 300 and 400 yards. In open country, shots at those ranges might be the best that muleys will offer.

Where to hit muleys is debatable. It depends largely on the pose your buck assumes at critical moments. Considering the probable ranges, I'd suggest that a novice study pictured poses of deer in all possible positions. The main thing is to get that bullet through the vitals without shooting up any significant amount of eating meat. Make it a rule to take the solidest possible shooting position; never shoot offhand if you can kneel or sit or even take a rest which approximates the solidity of the prone position. At long range you can't afford wobbles in your shooting iron. It's foolish to try for pinpoint hits if you can hold for the biggest fatal target of all, the lung area, but care shouldn't stop there. You should try to place your bullet in the center of that lung area, thus allowing for some error in judging range and wind deflection.

What rifle should you use? I know of no modern-day caliber that far surpasses the venerable .270 for plains hunting. Sure, some of the Magnums are a bit better but there are many other calibers a lot less suitable. The man with an accurate .270 needn't take a back seat to anyone toting a .308, .30/06, 7×57mm, or any other calibers below the 7mm Magnum or .300 Magnum. In the hands of a good shot and a capable hunter, the .243 Winchester or 6mm Remington may be rifle enough, but I prefer something spitting heavier than 100-grain bullets, both to hold up in velocity and to buck wind over normal muley-hunting ranges. The deer cartridges I would *not* choose for this open country are those of looping trajectory, such as the .44 Magnum, the .444, and even the revived .45/70.

Grain-fed mule deer get plenty of antler-building minerals in the rich grass-lands. This example is a magnificent nontypical trophy from the Province of Alberta. (Photo: Bert Popowski)

Having mentioned antelope in connection with range, I should add that the hunter of grain-belt muleys has a sporting bonus: a wide variety of game that's fattening up to survive winter or to fuel migrations. Early deer seasons range from late September to late October, the very same months when all other wildlife is conditioning itself for the lean cold months to come. Nonresident nimrods frequently encounter bonanzas of such early migrants as mourning doves and teal. These are trailed by the larger waterfowl, plus local crops of upland game, including the historic prairie chickens and burly sage grouse. I've guided some visiting hunters who lived off lesser game they harvested as windfalls of muley scouting trips before the deer seasons opened. Some of them even became acquainted with my favorite of all Western big game, the speedy pronghorn antelope, in those trans-Mississippi states which permit visiting hunters to pursue this species.

Where to hunt grain-belt muleys depends on which areas are cropped with small grains and legumes or are devoted to raising livestock. Many parts of some Western states were naturally arid but have been salvaged by a checkerboarding of impounded waters for irrigation and a jigsawing of diverted runoff to fill livestock dams or reservoirs. Where these make the soil bloom, they are natural magnets for muleys and other wildlife. But the crop-growing season is short. Thus western North Dakota, with the potential of tapping the Missouri River impoundments, will steadily improve its grain-belt muley production. It now harvests some 4,500 head, approximately 25 percent of its estimated muley breeding stock.

Kansas operates at about the same success ratio but confines its deer hunting to resident hunters. Nebraska and South Dakota do somewhat better, out of herds of approximately 85,000 muleys each on their western prairie lands. About 70 percent of their resident and visiting hunters fill their licenses.

The next tier of Western states, beginning with Montana and running through Wyoming and Colorado, are lavish muley producers. No clear-cut segregation can be made in the location of grain-belt and mountain muleys, though obviously the former are more easterly in the three states. Locally, it depends on where natural flatlands occur to allow farming and irrigation. Some of those croplands extend clear to the immense wheatlands of eastern Oregon and Washington, with occasional patches in south-central Idaho. Wherever they exist, muleys fatten on them. Even whitetails have been transplanted to some of these areas in the continuing experimental introduction of game species into areas of suitable habitat. Our excise-tax moneys, derived from the sale of guns and ammunition, pay for such introductions through game department interstate horse trading.

It should be noted that many Western states have extensive Indian Reservations on which human disturbance is about as light as on national grasslands and national forests. Some reservation lands are leased for cropping and running livestock, but this doesn't void hunting rights. These remain under tribal ownership and require the payment of trespass and/or hunting fees to the Tribal Council. Many reservations also require the use of Indian guides for visiting hunters.

All in all, hunting grain-belt muleys calls for more initiative than most other forms of deer hunting because so many variables can change from spot to spot according to the time of day, the quality of habitat, the kind of terrain, and the amount of human harassment. All deer are supposed to be nocturnal. But if considerable distances separate muley bedding

Oglala Rangers Sammy Cook (left) and Johnny Swallow proudly show a mule deer taken by the author. They guided him to this buck at one of his favorite grain-belt hunting places, the Pine Ridge Reservation. (Photo: Bert Popowski)

grounds from feeding areas, muleys will be late getting home in the morning and start out during daylight to feed throughout the night. Conversely, if their habitat provides food and shelter close together, muleys may bed down within a few hundred yards of where they fill their paunches. If the vegetation suits them and is undisturbed, they may lie up within neck's length of grub. So—whether on or off a reservation—a guide may be a big help to someone who isn't acquainted with the habits of the deer in a particular grain-belt muley haven.

17

The West Coast's Elusive Columbian Blacktails

by Norm Nelson

Remember the story about Cinderella? Her problem wasn't lack of beauty and grace and charm—it was just that no one on the home front really appreciated her.

This is much the case with the Columbian blacktail, that dark brown wraith of the Pacific Coast forest country. Three Western states, Washington, Oregon, and California, have high populations of them. But in a good part of his range, the blacktail tends to be under-appreciated and under-hunted.

Take my home state of Washington. Better than two-thirds of the state's three million people live west of the Cascade crest, which is where the blacktails live, too. But every year, tens of thousands of western Washington hunters hie themselves over the mountain passes to hunt mule deer in the arid western uplands, while lots of prime blacktail hunting goes begging closer to home.

The reason, of course, is that muleys in open pine forests or range country are much easier to hunt. But the difficulty of taking him is one part of the blacktail's appeal. A good blacktail buck rates as a real trophy, antler size notwithstanding, in terms of hunter achievement.

Until recent times, the blacktail was classified as a distinct species. Now, however, the biological pundits have demoted the blacktail to just a subspecies of the closely related mule deer. But to the hunter, the Columbian blacktail is a far different deer, unique unto himself. His habits and habitat are just as different from a mule deer's as the blacktail's substantial tail brush is different from the muley's tiny posterior rope. Conventional mule-deer tactics simply aren't relevant to hunting blacktails.

The blacktail is not a daily long-distance commuter as many muleys are. A mule deer may feed in a valley bottom at night and bed in daytime

A blacktail hunter glasses a timbered draw in a Pacific Northwest forest. Columbian blacktail deer are found in several kinds of habitat, but country like this qualifies, nevertheless, as typical. (Photo: Norm Nelson)

one to three miles distant, up in high, rocky country offering the cover he craves. By contrast, the blacktail often has his bedroom and dining room in the same piece of forest. And in the rainier portions of his coastal range, he need not travel far to find water.

Chew on that information a bit, and think hard. Get the point? Forest blacktails don't have to move about very much in their day-to-day life-support activities. And any deer that doesn't have to expose himself moving around is a lot tougher to hunt. His vulnerability to the sharp-eyed, listening hunter, who may be prowling or standing at a

A hunter scouts a clear-cut that has already become blanketed with trailing blackberry between the stems of Douglas fir that are starting to sprout. Since trailing blackberry is a prime deer food, and it's growing near excellent cover, the hunter knows he's in a promising area. (Photo: Norm Nelson)

deer trail junction, is drastically reduced. That's only part of the problem. When the blacktail does stir his stumps and start moving, he's likely to be traveling through the damnedest jungles you'll find this side of equatorial regions. I grew up hunting whitetails in the thick brush and post-fire, second-growth forests of northern Minnesota and thought I knew what thick cover was—until I moved to the Pacific Northwest. Here, typical blacktail habitat is likely to be incredibly thick, young evergreens, close-spaced red alder, clumps of devil's club and sprawling vine maple, myrtle, or ferns that grow 6 feet high. A blacktail slinking through that cover is almost invisible much of the time. So would be an elephant!

Late one afternoon last fall, I picked a good stump covering deer trails in the 387,000-acre Clemons Tree Farm of the Weyerhaeuser Company in western Washington. In the last 30 minutes of shooting time, I heard the light shuffle of a deer wading fetlock deep through the stiff-leaved salal and cascara. Unfortunately, it didn't take quite the right trail and missed me by 20 feet, about the distance of a good living room's span, or close enough to take him with a fast bayonet charge, right? No dice. The deer was so thoroughly screened in doghair-thick baby hemlock that I never saw him, although I found droppings still at body temperature a couple of minutes later.

Thus, the blacktail is a very hard quarry to hang on a gambrel stick. That's not because he's super-smart, as Eastern whitetails have become after two centuries of white man's hunting. It's because the blacktail's coastal forest habitat gives him a big advantage over the invading human hunter.

Even so, the cause is not hopeless. Tens of thousands of blacktails are taken annually in California, Oregon, and Washington (not to mention British Columbia and the Alaskan panhandle, home of the smaller Sitka

It's sometimes said that blacktails favor a mixture of timber and openings such as clear-cuts, but that's a simplification. For example, one of their favorite haunts is this kind of dense lowland thicket of red alder. Still-hunting a stretch of brush and tangles like this would be just as difficult as still-hunting a brushy Eastern woodlot. (Photo: Norm Nelson)

These blacktail does are feeding in a clear-cut area. The Pacific Northwest has many such spots where Columbian blacktails come to browse. (Photo: Norm Nelson)

blacktail). It helps to know more about the blacktail's ecology. Like his forest-dwelling peer, the whitetail, the Columbian blacktail does best in a ''disturbed environment.'' Ancient virgin forests, untouched by man or natural catastrophe, have little or no food to offer the blacktail, and you'll rarely find him there.

A naturalist at the turn of the century, D. G. Elliot, spent five weeks in Washington's Olympic Mountains, virgin wilderness then and now, to take museum specimens. ''Although we hunted continually,'' Elliot reported, ''no elk were seen while we remained at this camp, and deer, the true blacktail, the only species found in these mountains, were very scarce, and we only succeeded in obtaining a doe and a fawn. . . . I do not think I was ever before in a country that was apparently so devoid of animal life.''

The problem is that thick forest shuts off sunlight from the forest floor. This drastically reduces the amount of brush and other browse. In turn, this means no game. However, blacktails historically could be found in places where major fires swept away an old-growth forest. This was one reason why coastal Indians did some primitive game management in the form of semi-controlled burning. Some of the "natural" prairies that settlers found in western Washington resulted from repeated burning by the Indians to provide clearings in which the camas lily, a staple food of theirs, was able to grow. These clearings also provided brush, low plants, and grasses to attract and maintain elk and deer populations.

Like the whitetail, the blacktail, where he could be found, was decimated by uncontrolled settler meat hunting. But, again like the whitetail, better days were coming for the surviving blacktails. Careless settlers' forest fires and the start of logging in the Northwest began to provide blacktail habitat that simply didn't exist in the untouched forest. The dominant Douglas fir here is best harvested by clear-cutting in blocks, since fir seedlings for the next forest generation need full sunlight. For several years after harvest, these clear-cuts provide a food-supply paradise for blacktails (plus elk, grouse, and band-tailed pigeons).

In a clear-cut, sunlight is available to quickly cover the logged-off area with trailing blackberry, huckleberry, young vine maple, and other low plants on which blacktails can thrive the year around. Of course, as the clear-cut is restocked with seedling trees, either by man or nature, it eventually grows back into a forest dense enough once more to shut off that sunlight-generated food supply. But that will take a few years, even with today's speeded-up planting by the forest industry. And by the time a former clear-cut becomes too overgrown with young timber to supply much deer food any longer, there will be other rotational harvest areas in the same neighborhood to supply new browse areas.

So, the overall picture for the blacktail is a bright one. Although effective fire suppression today means that nature no longer is doing much clear-cutting for the benefit of deer and other wildlife, perpetual-yield logging harvests are providing the same benefit without fire's wildlife casualties and possible loss of soil fertility in severe burns.

For the blacktail hunter, the obvious lesson is: Go not to an old-growth, Walt Disney/Sierra Club forest, but find an area that has had repeated logging activity in various spots during recent years.

Washington Game Department researchers list four stages of forest succession. These are clues to good deer hunting. Stage 1 involves recently logged or burned areas where existing vegetation is presently grasses and forbs (nonshrub, low-growing plants). Deer frequent these areas in late summer and early fall, particularly if there is a good stand of fireweed. However, in Stage 1 succession, there are not enough of the browse shrub species available yet to provide late-fall and winter forage. Don't expect deer to be in one of these relatively new clear-cuts or burns in October simply because you saw blacktails there in August.

In Stage 2, the prominent vegetation has become shrubs. As the Washington Game Department's excellent book on blacktail research put it, "These [Stage 2] areas are approaching the peak productivity of deer forage and the forage produced is of high quality."

Later, in Stage 3, dominant vegetation has become second-growth coniferous or deciduous tree species. overshadowing the shrubs to some extent. Finally, in Stage 4 the timber species have grown big enough to allow only a few shade-tolerant shrub species, ferns, and a few forbs to exist. This is poor foraging for deer, but animals will use such an area for bedding or escape cover.

Therefore, a blacktail hunter does well if he starts by looking for country *with a combination of Stage 2, Stage 3, and Stage 4 areas*. Weed-overgrown clearings of Stage 2 provide plenty of food for blacktails. But except at the beginning of the season, a hunter may not catch deer well out in such open terrain. They often browse after dark.

Stage 3 sites have both the groceries for blacktails and somewhat better cover. During daylight hours, deer are likeliest to be either in the best cover features of Stage 3 land or in Stage 4 forests immediately adjoining Stage 2 and Stage 3 areas. Anywhere you find this diversity of sites in blacktail country, you are practically certain to find deer or lacking that, at least deer signs.

A logical scheme for hunting under these conditions would be to start before daybreak by taking a stand at a downwind vantage point overlooking a clear-cut several years old—that is, either Stage 2 or Stage 3 land. Good binoculars are vital here. At shooting light, watch carefully along the edges of a clear-cut or old burn for deer drifting slowly back into the adjoining thicker forest cover.

If there is a lot of forest debris in the form of discarded limbs, tree tops, or burn snags, it can be tough to see the dark brown forms of blacktails threading their way through this slash. It can be even more difficult to make out antlers, which is why binoculars are strongly recommended.

The blacktail has some quirks of his own. Like the mule deer, the blacktail often travels along the face or crest of a ridge, something that whitetails often are not too keen to do. But while a frightened muley often runs uphill to even higher ground, a startled blacktail will usually dive through the timber downhill. His aim is to get into the densest creek-bottom cover. In the rainy Cascades and Olympics, every valley has some kind of water course at the bottom. Along the creeks, thick stands of alder, vine maple, and some red cedar provide better cover than the more open timber on the hillsides. Blacktails know this very well.

If a drive is planned using standers and drivers, care must be taken to cover both the creek bottom and the hillsides. There is no guarantee which route a blacktail will use, moving out ahead of the drivers. If he's not too spooked and figures he has the situation well in hand, he may stay on the face of a ridge working a hundred yards or more ahead of the

Here's the famous Columbian blacktail of Washington, Oregon, and California. All three states have healthy populations of this mule-deer subspecies, but that doesn't mean it's easy—or common—to get a close standing shot at a prime buck like this. Just as in other regions, you have to scout the habitat. (Photo: Leonard Lee Rue IV)

drivers. If badly worried, he'll be sneaking through the thickest cover he can find down in the creek bottom. Of course, like other deer, he'll be traveling upwind.

Blacktails are as surefooted as Rocky Mountain mule deer and can negotiate steep hillsides. Since they live in heavy cover a good part of the time, they are not averse to traveling through the densest kind of thickets that even the cover-loving whitetail would tend to detour.

Obviously a blacktail hunter has problems in flat country due to the lack of visibility typical of the coastal forest. For this reason, chances are better when hunting on ridges. My preference is for country that is not too steep. This allows me to spend more time looking for deer either ahead on my ridge or on the face of an adjoining parallel ridge. In really steep terrain, one must spend too much time watching his footing and picking a route, instead of concentrating on looking for deer.

I also prefer a country with small water courses. This means that the paralleling ridges on each side of such a creek will be fairly close with a better chance of an in-range shot at a deer on the opposite side of a draw or a canyon.

In contrasting three decades or more of whitetail-hunting experience with almost a decade of blacktail hunting, it's my conviction that the blacktail is not as predictable in bad weather as a whitetail. When it rains, a whitetail can be counted on to move into the best of available cover, such as dense evergreens. But the blacktail is used to rain and will not necessarily hole up. He would starve if he did, since it rains pretty steadily for five months of the year in the coastal Northwest. Therefore, the hunter is as likely to find blacktails in the more open forest as in heavy cover, even though it may be raining.

Although blacktails range high into the mountains during the summer and early fall, snow will drive them down to the valleys. A hunter in the right place can take advantage of this, working to intercept movements of deer immediately before or after a snow storm in the high country.

The gorgeous mountain country of the Northwest is certainly the most scenic area for blacktail hunting, but don't overlook lowland forests bordering agricultural country. Like whitetails, blacktails have thrived on man's agricultural practices. Woodlot hunting in Northwest lowland farm country produces some fine bucks, since these tend to be better-fed than their hardscrabble brethren up on the rocky mountainsides. Down in California, blacktails tend to become serious agricultural pests. Like mule deer wrecking young alfalfa, blacktails tend to graze in the manner of sheep, lipping off clover and trefoil so close to the ground that the plants never recover. They also raise hob with young nut trees, prune shoots, and grape tendrils in the Golden State. And like whitetails, blacktails can live in wooded suburban areas, alternating forest foods with goodies out of gardens. I've seen them dash across roadways at night in a city of 150,000 population.

From north to south, blacktail hunting techniques don't vary greatly. The California hunter jump-shooting deer in hillside patches of oak and brush is following the same approach as the Oregon or Washington hunter threading through hillside timber in the hope of spotting a running buck on the opposite ravine slope. While the Northwesterner may try stand-hunting a forest clear-cut at dawn, the Californian may be glassing an agricultural field at daybreak; the strategies are the same.

Hunting conditions vary a lot, however. Early-season blacktail hunting in California can be a 100-degree affair with heat mirage shimmering the chamiso and sage hills. Farther north, the blacktail hunter assumes he is going to hunt wet. There is no escaping it; he will soon be soaked in the rain-drenched autumn forest, just from wet foliage alone, even if the day dawns clear after a typical night's drizzle.

The hot-weather blacktail hunter's garb is simple—something cool like a tee shirt, jeans, and a wide-brimmed hat. The Northern forest hunter had best wear wool. In time, it will get wet on him, but even wet wool has some heat-retaining value in cool weather. And blacktail hunting can be cool in October and November in the Northwest. Light bird boots may be best for the warm-zone hunter, but in the Northwest timber, lug soles of stiff rubber can be essential to avoid bad falls on wet forest debris. One hunter I know who is also a logger wears his sharp-spiked logging boots when hunting a favorite area with lots of blowdown timber. With his "corks" (a corruption of "caulks"), he can often travel a hundred yards at a time, silent and sure-footed as a stalking cougar, atop fallen fir and hemlock, often 6 to 10 feet above the ground.

Blacktail rifles offer an interesting problem. On the face of it, a Northwest hunter would be best off with a fast-handling lever, pump, or autoloader of moderate power. The Eastern whitetail hunter's classic .30/30 lever gun would appear perfect. And for a lot of blacktail hunting, a rifle of that genre is great.

But blacktail country and blacktails are unpredictable. A flat-topped, dense forest ridge may open up into a series of draws and canyons that offer shooting out to 300 yards or more on farther slopes. A powerful, accurate bolt-action rifle would be the ticket here, if it wears at least 4× in scope magnification. But, believe me, such a "Long Ranger" is practically useless in dense forest and brush.

So a compromise is called for. My choice would be an autoloader,

Blacktail shots often call for a scope, but just as often iron sights have the advantage. The author therefore likes this type of rig—a scope in a Pachmayr Lo-Swing side mount, plus iron sights. (Photo: Norm Nelson)

For quite a while the author kept his blacktail rifle mounted with a 3×–9× variable scope, as seen here—and it obviously did its job well. These days, however, Nelson uses a slightly lower-powered replacement, a 2×–7× variable. (Photo: Norm Nelson)

pump, or lever-action. Caliber choice would be .308 or .30/06 with the longer, cross-canyon shots in mind. The need for a cartridge with power for versatility rules out the guns available only for close or mid-range cartridges like the .30/30 or .35 Remington.

Only as a last resort do I want a bolt-action for *timber*. Shots here tend to be often at fast-running game. Trees and brush conceal the target part of the time, offering only snapshot opportunities in natural "holes" in the forest cover. The faster a shooter can reload his chamber with minimum distraction or movement of his rifle from the shoulder, the better he can concentrate on the lightning-reflex business of picking a clear spot for a snapshot at fleeing game. With this in mind, the autoloader is best, the pump action is almost as good, the lever gun less so, and the bolt-action the worst of the lot. While damnable heresy to today's bolt-action cult, that's just the way it is down in the timber and puckerbrush, like it or not!

I recommend the .30-calibers for blacktail hunting because of overlaps with elk seasons in Oregon and Washington, plus the chance of collecting a big bonus black bear in these states. Those factors rule out something like the .243 even though it is certainly adequate on blacktails.

Sighting equipment calls for as much thoughtful choice as the rifle. Iron sights would be okay in the thickets but no good for the clear-cuts or the canyon shots. The logical choice is a variable-power scope, 2–7× or even 1½–4×. The lower settings offer plenty of wide field for timber work, while the higher settings do the business on long-shot opportunities. The modern tapered crosshairs, thick through most of their span but tapering at the junction, are probably the best compromise. Standard crosshairs can be too hard to pick up in dark timber, dot reticles are far too small for close-range snapshooting, and post reticles can be too coarse for long-range chances.

I personally favor the Pachmayr Lo-Swing mounts and have these on three of my favorite rifles. Even waterproof scopes of high quality can develop air leaks, leading to fogging in the wet forests. The tough woods-walking can lead to bone-wrenching falls that leave you wondering if your scope is still sighted in. Under either of those conditions—and I have had them happen several times—it's nice to be able to flip the mount over, leaving a good set of iron sights open to the eye without obstruction. In chronically wet woods, I simply unscrew the mount's center hinge collar and put the scope in my daypack, using iron sights until things dry out. Even an unfogged scope can be rendered semi-useless by water smears on the optics and smears of this sort simply can't be prevented in dripping brush cover.

A good compass plus some basic understanding of the area is essential for forest blacktail hunting in the Northwest. These are big woods where a man, once lost, might never show up again. A decent pack is good for carrying rain gear while stump-sitting (but it will be too hot and noisy to wear if you're continually on the move). Also, a pack is dandy for packing out a boned and quartered buck on the day when you shoot one a mile back in some appalling blowdown that prevents dragging out the buck in one piece.

Blacktails vary greatly in size, depending upon region. In California, a blacktail buck will weigh from 60 to not over 100 pounds, dressed. Farther north, the Columbian variety can run from 150 up to 200 pounds, although the latter would be uncommon. Still farther north, the Sitka subspecies again is a small deer.

Blacktail racks are disappointing if matched with the awesome spread of a Rocky Mountain mule deer or the heavy-beamed, forward sweep of a Northern whitetail buck. Spikes and forks are common on blacktails, and three-pointers are considered very "skookum" indeed. Once in a while, a hunter clobbers a really big, prime Northwest blacktail with four or five points on a side. This may well be a trophy of a lifetime and should be caped and handled as such for good taxidermy work; you may never get one like it in your sights again.

Where to hunt? Picking a general area is the least of your problems. As cited earlier, blacktails tend to be underhunted in much of their range. In northern California, Oregon, and Washington, plenty of federal forests and timber-company lands are open to all comers who behave themselves.

As always, preseason scouting, if possible, greatly enhances your chances. Pioneering a new area, it's a good idea to look up the local wildlife agent or biologist for specific information. In recent years, temporary blacktail scarcities existed after die-offs due to freakishly severe winter conditions. Blacktails are not as winter-hardy as Northern muleys and whitetails. As of 1975, however, herds have largely recovered in places where winter loss occurred a few years earlier. The blacktail's future is bright. Stepped-logging rotations in coastal forest country mean more good blacktail habitat in years to come. The main management problem with blacktails in many areas is overpopulation, paired with underharvest of the deer. Such biopolitical shortsightedness contributed in no small part to the bad starvation losses in the tough winters of the late 1960s.

The author has been lucky enough to have lived in a variety of fine deer country, ranging from the Lake States to the Pacific Northwest. I've hunted and taken whitetails, muleys, and blacktails. Each has its own charm and challenge. Nothing tests the hunter's woodcraft and alertness like a whitetail in his typical habitat. That magnificent mountaineer, the Rocky Mountain mule deer, requires strong legs, good lungs, and shooting ability from the hunter. The blacktail offers his share of all these challenges. Hunting him can combine the best demands of both whitetails and muleys. That's why a good blacktail buck is my personal choice of a most-wanted deer trophy.

18

Strange Ways of the Northwest's Sitka Blacktails

by Don McKnight

Although Alaska is better known for Dall sheep, moose, caribou, and big bears, its Sitka blacktail deer provide some of the finest hunting to be had anywhere on the North American continent. With five-month seasons and limits of four deer per year, it is a deer hunter's dream come true. Where else are 60 to 70 percent success rates common and where else do 15 to 20 percent of licensed hunters kill four deer per year?

This little deer can be distinguished from its cousin the Columbian blacktail by its smaller size and short-legged, chunky appearance. An occasional exceptionally large buck may dress out at 200 pounds, but over much of the range the average mature buck will rarely exceed 100 to 120 pounds, field-dressed.

Antlers are relatively small, few scoring 110 points under the Boone & Crockett system. Yearlings and two-year-olds often wear only un-branched spikes. Branched antlers occur by the third year. Fully de-veloped antlers on a mature buck may have four or five points per side, including a long brow tine (eye-guard). More typically, however, mature bucks carry only a fork on each side.

The Sitka blacktail originally was limited in distribution to the coastal rain forests from the Queen Charlotte Islands off the British Columbia coast north through the islands and mainland comprising the Southeastern Alaska Panhandle. The northern portion of the range includes the "ABC" (Admiralty, Baranof, and Chichagof) Islands, where this deer and the Alaskan brown bear are the only native big-game animals (goats were transplanted to Baranof Island in 1923). On islands farther south, wolves and black bears share blacktail habitat, and all four species plus mountain goats inhabit the mainland. Thus a sportsman can combine his pursuit of the blacktail with a hunt for other Alaskan species, and a "mixed-bag" expedition for big game can be a memorable experience.

From 1916 through 1923 Sitka blacktails were captured on southeastern Alaska islands and transported to several islands in Prince William Sound near Cordova. These transplants, and several later ones to Kodiak Island and the Yakutat area, were successful and the species now provides hunting in these areas as well.

Sitka blacktail numbers, like those of most herbivores (plant-eaters) at the northern fringe of their range, fluctuate greatly from year to year. During a severe winter, heavy snow accumulations for prolonged periods result in major losses through starvation, and herds may be depleted by 30 to 60 percent. Several successive severe winters (as occurred during the early 1970s) leave deer numbers at very low levels. These little deer are extremely prolific, however, as demonstrated by a yearling doe shot last fall by a friend of mine. She was accompanied by a nearly grown fawn at the time and was about to ovulate twin ova—in all likelihood she would have given birth to three fawns before reaching the age of two years. It is not hard to see how deer numbers can rebound quickly when coastal Alaska is blessed with several mild winters in a row.

Stands of old-growth spruce and hemlock along beaches are the key to winter survival for this species throughout its range. Even though temperatures along Alaska's coast are moderated by the influence of the Japanese Current, snow accumulations even at sea level can be substantial. Under the closed canopy of spruces and hemlocks, snow depths are less than in the open and deer can find enough twigs (mostly from blueberry bushes) and forbs, augmented by summer-stored fat supplies, to ensure survival. It is when snows pile up 4 or 5 feet deep even under these trees that winter losses become extreme.

Each spring, as snows recede with warming temperatures, Sitka blacktails begin to drift up to higher elevations. With nearly limitless supplies of high-quality food on alpine ranges (mostly low-growing herbs), they wax fat by the end of summer.

This generalized scheme of things is complicated by several factors. Obviously snowfall and snow accumulation vary between portions of the Sitka blacktail's range. In southeastern Alaska, more southerly areas receive less snow than those farther north. Islands along the outer coast, because of the influence of ocean temperatures, receive less snow than islands farther east. Deer herds at Yakutat and on the islands of Prince William Sound are heavily impacted by deep snows.

On some islands and much of the southeast Alaska mainland, wolves are a major predator of deer. Herds in these areas seem to recover from population lows more slowly than those on islands where wolves are not found. In addition, clear-cut logging practices on national forest lands in southeastern Alaska have had a detrimental impact on the area's deer

A hunter poses with a nice Sitka blacktail taken on a warm, typically misty day. This buck was small enough for an easy drag to the beach, but he provided plenty of good venison.

herds. Timber removal results in increased browse production but during the critical winter months all food may be covered with snow. The dependence of these deer on old-growth, beach-fringe timber—which is attractive to the timber industry—is their biggest problem for the future.

Although annual deer-hunting seasons and limits in Alaska vary somewhat because of fluctuations in deer numbers, generally speaking the hunter can expect open seasons somewhere in the state anytime between August 1 and December 31. Limits over much of its range are four deer per year, with both bucks and does legal after September 15.

During August and early September most large bucks are on their alpine summer ranges and the hunter must plan on at least an overnight trip, hiking to about timberline, setting up a hasty camp, then hunting the high, open slopes. Weather can limit the opportunities to enjoy an alpine hunt—rarely do late summer rains cease for the few days necessary. Timberline occurs at from 1,000 to 2,500 feet in most deer country, and with few trails or roads through the dense undergrowth such a hunt is only for those in good physical condition. Many hunters dress their animal and bone out its meat on the spot to minimize the weight they must pack on the treacherous and tiring descent.

Rewards of such a hunt are many. Alpine scenery and the view of surrounding fiords and timbered islands are breathtaking and the hunter will generally see many deer and other forms of wildlife. Because of the open terrain, a flat-shooting rifle equipped with a good scope is recommended. (I'll have more to say in a few moments about appropriate blacktail rifles for the lowlands and in bear country.)

Alpine hunting, although an excellent way to enjoy the Sitka blacktail and his country, is not a very efficient method of meat-gathering, and most of the annual harvest occurs during the months of November and December. As the season's first frosts kill alpine vegetation and October snows force deer to lower elevations, local deer hunters start to think seriously of filling their larders. Beginning in early November, deer are concentrated at lower elevations, visibility is better because most shrubs and bushes have lost their leaves, and the rut makes the animals less wary and therefore more vulnerable to hunting. (To the bear-shy hunter, another advantage is that by this time of the year many brownies have denned up for the winter in the high country now covered by snow.)

The wise hunter wastes little time hunting areas near the beach. He knows that most Sitka blacktails will be concentrated at or slightly above

Here are two hog-fat bucks and a doe near the edge of an alpine meadow. The author notes that on clear, hot days (rare during the season) Sitka blacktails tend to congregate in spots like this—near snow patches where they can stay cool and where insects are less of a nuisance than in the warmer parts of the habitat.

the snowline, moving to lower elevations only as snows accumulate to depths exceeding their tolerances. With each new snowfall the deer will move downhill to elevations where warmer temperatures result in rain rather than snow. As the snow stops and warming temperatures melt accumulations at low levels, deer will push back uphill, always staying as high as possible. Some of the easiest hunting occurs on a morning following a night of heavy snow right down to the beachline. Deer, concentrated along the beach fringe, will not yet have begun moving back to higher elevations; they can be tracked successfully and are easier to distinguish against the white background.

It is also in November and December that the Sitka deer hunter's biggest "ace in the hole"—his deer call—can be used most effectively. Aside from the mostly Southwestern technique of antler-rattling, the notion of calling deer is probably new and strange to most hunters below the Canadian border. But for some unknown reason, Sitka blacktails of both sexes at times respond spectacularly to the loud bleats produced in calling. Some believe deer come to a call out of curiosity or that it resembles the distress cry of a fawn. I'm becoming more and more convinced, however, that these diminutive deer use vocalizations as an additional means for getting bucks and does together during the rutting season. Regardless of why it works, calling is a very effective and often exciting means of putting venison in the freezer.

Although a few of my deer-hunting acquaintances successfully call deer using the old Tlingit Indian trick of blowing through a blade of grass placed over their clenched thumbs, most hunters prefer to use a commercially manufactured call or one they have made themselves. In the past few years one sporting-goods dealer has been selling all of the commercial quail calls he can put on the shelf; these calls produce a high-pitched bleat which is seemingly irresistible to Sitka deer. Some commercial predator calls appear to be equally good, although I haven't tried one yet. I make my own by placing a rubber band between two notched sticks, then wrapping their ends with friction tape.

The secret of successful calling can be summed up in one word—perseverance. A deer might rush right up to the hunter before he can return the call to his pocket, but it is much more likely to sneak toward the source of the call, taking 10 to 15 minutes to arrive. I'm convinced that calling will work only under the following circumstances: First, the deer has not scented the caller; and second, the deer is near enough to hear the call. The second certainly is obvious enough but therein lies the limitation to the successes achieved by the caller. These deer have an excellent sense of smell, and unless conditions are perfect they can scent you as quickly as they can hear you. Dripping rain and many burbling streams at this time of the year dampen sound, and even a loud bleat can be heard

Too many sportsmen have the erroneous notion that meager winter browse is a problem only in the Eastern states where human development has drastically reduced the deer habitat. These three Sitka blacktails of southeastern Alaska are severely winter-weakened. The author believes they had little chance of surviving until spring. McKnight stresses that management programs are necessary wherever deer herds are to be maintained in good condition.

only a short distance in these conditions. I've found calls to be completely useless on windy days, perhaps because the wind wafts my scent to the deer more readily or perhaps because it is too noisy for them to hear the call.

For late-season hunting many, including myself, successfully combine still-hunting with calling to get their deer. By walking quietly with many stops and much looking, particularly at dawn and just before dusk, it is possible to spot deer that are moving to and from bedding areas. At other times of day, when deer are holed up in the brush in their beds, calling will produce when still-hunting is futile. Deer are found in scattered groups at this time of year, so walk until you find fresh sign. Then poke around slowly, with a sharp eye peeled (always walking into any breeze). If this doesn't produce, pick a place with unimpaired visibility in all or most directions, make yourself comfortable, and call. Some people use several loud bleats followed up in 10 minutes or so with a couple more. I use a series of three long and two short blasts. Remain quietly in place for at least 15 minutes, carefully scanning the surrounding area for an inquisitive eye or out-of-place leg or back. Bucks, particularly, will sneak up to the source of the call, figure out they've been hoodwinked, and sneak away without being seen. I've listened to deer work all the way around my location until they got my scent and departed without my ever being able to see them.

On the other hand, I've stood in the middle of an open muskeg, called, and had a deer dash out of the brush right up to me, stopping at 20 feet to eye this strange creature standing on its hind legs. Another time, I walked into an opening, seated myself comfortably on a stump, and called,

This buck, taken on Montague Island in Prince William Sound, is an extremely fine specimen of the Sitka blacktail. Field-dressed, he weighed 186 pounds.

ignoring the wood-edge through which I had walked on the assumption that no deer would respond from that direction. After about 10 minutes some instinct made me look over my shoulder—right into the eyes of an inquisitive buck standing head-down 30 feet away.

A word of warning to those hunting Sitka blacktails where brown bears are found: They, too, will respond to a deer call. I know of one southeastern Alaska hunter whose throat constricts involuntarily whenever he attempts to blow his deer call in bear country. It seems he once had a huge old brownie come running to his call, and was lucky enough to kill it with one shot at approximately 10 yards. Several years ago another fellow, hunting deer, shot a wolverine that came to his call.

This leads us to a discussion of firearms for use on Sitka blacktails. These little deer are easy to kill and my favorite rifle for them is a .222 weighing about 6½ pounds with its 1¾× scope. Like many Alaska hunters, however, I refuse to shoot at a running deer, preferring a head or neck shot at a motionless animal. This way very little meat is lost. Unfortunately, most of my hunting is done in areas where there is a possibility of confronting a hungry or angry brown bear. In such areas I forsake the little .222 for the security of a heavier caliber. Several of my hunting companions feel comfortable in bear country only when toting their favorite .375 or .458 Magnum, relying on loaded-down cartridges and head or neck shots to reduce destruction of choice meat. I originally did my bear-country deer hunting with a .300 H&H Magnum, the heaviest caliber in my arsenal, but when several years passed without bear problems I reverted to an old favorite .270. This rifle, equipped with a 4× scope and weighing nearly 10 pounds, is an old friend that has killed many head of big game, but its weight makes it anything but the ideal deer rifle in southeastern Alaska. Most shots are at stationary animals at ranges of less than 50 yards and any lightweight rifle of heavy enough caliber to stop a bear in an emergency would be adequate. Because of the constant problem of keeping a scope dry in the rain and wet brush, a receiver sight would be ideal. Those who must use a scope will find several waterproof scope covers on the market. Few hunters as yet have challenged these deer with bow and arrow, but the opportunities are great.

Rainy weather and moderate temperatures prevail throughout the hunting season, and wool clothing, which retains warmth in spite of being wet, is worn by most Alaskan deer hunters. Conventional rubberized rain parkas and rain pants will keep you drier but most hunters prefer to sacrifice comfort for stealth and wear only a waterproof hat with their wool clothing. Footgear most commonly seen is a pair of "southeastern sandals"—knee-high, gum-rubber boots. For those who have trouble maintaining their bearings in cloudy or foggy weather, particularly in thick brush, a modest pocket compass is a necessary piece of equipment.

Following a light snowfall, this hunter took a small buck and, after field-dressing it, decided to carry it out to the beach pack-fashion. He removed the head to lighten the load and make it less awkward. For obvious reasons, McKnight does not recommend this procedure in any area where other hunters may be present. Even with the head removed, that buck might look too much like live game to a hunter just glimpsing a bit of it moving through cover.

Deer are plentiful within easy boating or hiking distance of most communities in the blacktail range, and often a successful hunt requires only a short walk or boat trip. Nevertheless, many hunters prefer the solitude provided by the numerous bays and coves far from towns. Air charter operations, using float-equipped small planes, are found in most coastal towns and provide an excellent means for getting to and from such areas. It must be remembered, however, that in Alaska it is illegal to hunt the same day you have flown to your hunting area.

The Forest Service maintains many rustic but comfortable cabins throughout southeastern Alaska and these are available on a reservation basis for a small fee.   Tents are also popular, but they should be double-walled or equipped with a rain fly to ensure dryness.

Perhaps the most enjoyable way to hunt, particularly late in the season, is to use a large boat as a base camp, traveling from bay to bay and hunting new country daily.   A variation of this is available in many communities, where local charter-boat operators offer one-day hunts.   They take out fifteen to twenty hunters before daylight, scatter them along the beach of a secluded bay, then pick them up at dusk.   For the $10 to $12 fee charged, this is one of the best hunting bargains available anywhere.   It used to be fashionable to hunt from a boat, cruising beachlines and shooting deer as they were seen.   This practice was considered to be less than sporting, however, and regulations were enacted which prohibit the shooting of any big-game animal except wolves from a boat in southeastern Alaska.

Visitors to Alaska wanting to hunt Sitka blacktails are not required to book a guide, but unless they are seasoned woodsmen a guide is advisable.   Boat-equipped guides reside in most southeastern communities and many of them take out parties of hunters for a week-long deer hunt at reasonable rates.   The multitude of commercial fishing boats at berth during the off-season provides another possibility for a hunt.   Chambers of commerce in most small towns would be a good contact for the prospective out-of-state deer hunter.   If the nonresident prefers to go it alone, a letter or phone call to any Alaska Department of Fish & Game office would provide information on good areas to hunt, and contact with a Forest Service office would reserve a cabin.   Aircraft charters are available with little advance notice.   A nonresident hunting license costs $20 in Alaska, and deer tags are $25 each.

Throughout its range in Alaska, the Sitka blacktail deer is an important source of meat for local residents.   Its venison has a fine texture and an unexcelled flavor.   Whether taken in high, open country during the early fall or in rain-drenched lowlands later in the season, this little deer offers a unique and memorable hunt.

Appendices

APPENDIX I

Range of Whitetail Deer and Mule Deer

by David Namias and Robert Elman

There are probably at least 20 million deer—and perhaps many more—in the United States and Canada.   In Chapter 13 on the various subspecies of whitetails, Leonard Lee Rue notes that the whitetail population in these two countries is currently estimated at more than 11 million (other estimates have gone as high as 16 million) and that at least one subspecies, the Northern whitetail (*Odocoileus virginianus borealis*), is increasing its numbers.   Many authorities agree that several other subspecies are also on the increase in a few more southerly regions.   The population of mule deer—including Columbian and Sitka blacktails—hovers between 7 and 8 million according to some estimates and tops 8 million according to others. Some of our best-informed wildlife biologists and game managers are convinced that all the estimates are conservative.   If we accept a figure of more than 8 million for mule deer and substantially more than 11 million for whitetails, a minimum total of 20 million deer seems reasonable.

The estimates fluctuate from region to region and from year to year, of course, depending on such factors as the severity of winter, competition from other species for the available browse—even animals as small as the gray squirrel affect the availability of mast and browse—and the destruction or improvement and occasional expansion of habitat.   Sharp or continuing increases in deer population are not always desirable, however. A population higher than the local habitat's carrying capacity eventually results in overbrowsing, excessive predation, crowding, malnutrition, birth defects, and so forth.   Ultimately such a population may plummet disastrously, as in the famous case of the Kaibab mule deer many years ago.   Or the deer may simply become stunted and unhealthy, a condition that can be seen right now in some of the Northeastern whitetail herds.

It is also true that in several regions the deer—particularly muleys—

WHITETAIL DISTRIBUTION

(Odocoileus virginianus)

The shaded portion of the map shows the primary range of whitetail deer. There are thirty recognized subspecies, distributed transcontinentally from central Canada to Panama. Of these, seventeen occur in Canada and the United States, and there are at least some whitetails in every one of the contiguous states. In parts of the Southeast, the population is so high that very generous bag limits and extended seasons are the rule. In parts of the Far West, however, there is no open season because the population is too sparse to be huntable. (See Chapter 13 on the various subspecies for notes on states with closed seasons.) In the Western regions that appear entirely barren on the map, the fringes of whitetail range are probably expanding—slowly and slightly—though in some parts of these regions they are dwindling. Whitetails are scarce in Oregon, southwestern Idaho, and northern Arizona, scarce or absent in large parts of Washington, California, Nevada, and Colorado. However, blacktails and other mule deer are plentiful in some of these areas—blacktails near the upper coast and the other mule deer farther inland.

MULE DEER DISTRIBUTION

(*Odocoileus hemionus*)

The shaded portion of the map shows the primary distribution of mule deer. The muleys in the upper Northwest are the Sitka and Columbian blacktail subspecies. The Sitka blacktail (*O. h. sitkensis*) ranges from southeastern Alaska into upper British Columbia (see Chapter 18) and the Columbian blacktail (*O. h. columbianus*) ranges from British Columbia down into California (see Chapter 17). Together they probably account for 1½ million of the 8 million or so mule deer. There are nine other recognized geographical races, or subspecies, according to some taxonomists, but many biologists lump them into fewer races because they tend to be so much alike. There are two main types—Rocky Mountain mule deer and the paler, smaller desert mule deer of Mexico and the deep Southwest. Within these two main types, the variations are so minor that they can be described as local adaptations to habitat. The total range extends from southeastern Alaska and the lower Yukon down into Northern Mexico and all of Mexico's Baja California peninsula, and from the Pacific Coast to the Plains States.

have been declining slightly in recent years, and bits of their traditional range have been sacrificed to man's activities, including just about everything from livestock grazing to highway building. But among mule deer, too, at least one subspecies, the Columbian blacktail (*Odocoileus hemionus columbianus*), is increasing its numbers and probably its range. (For additional details regarding current populations and the regional hunting outlook, see the Introduction.)

Generally speaking, the deer populations are higher than they were when the land was first settled, and the fringes of distribution shown on the accompanying range maps are slowly spreading in at least a few areas, although some areas of concentrated human activity within those ranges have been rendered almost barren of habitat. Fortunately, game management has become sufficiently sophisticated so that the future appears bright in spite of an inevitable destruction of range in regions where the human population is expected to become ever more dense.

APPENDIX 2

Field-Dressing, Hauling, Camp Care, Venison Viands, and Buckskin

by John Madson

FIELD-DRESSING AND HAULING

When your deer is down, never approach it closely until you are sure it is dead.   There are reliable reports of hunters being attacked by wounded bucks and finally killing the animals with belt knives.   One hunter straightened the head of his prize and laid his rifle in the antlers before taking a photograph.   He backed up, focused his camera, and looked up just in time to see the deer leap to his feet and disappear in the brush, rifle still hung from his antlers.

Many deer hunters use "sticking knives" whether the deer requires further bleeding or not.   If the animal has been hit in the head, neck, or spinal cord, bleeding may be necessary.   But if the wound is in lungs or heart and the deer has run for any distance, it may be almost "bled out" before you reach it.

To bleed a deer thoroughly, plunge your knife to the hilt at the junction of neck and chest, tilt the blade downward to the backbone, and withdraw it with a slight slicing effect.   This should sever the carotid arteries where they join midway between the shoulders.   When blood drainage has stopped, the next job is to remove the viscera as quickly and cleanly as possible.

Place the deer on its back on a slight slope or over a log or rock with the head uphill so that blood will drain to the hind parts.   With a very sharp knife—and keeping a whetstone handy—make your first cut along the center line of the belly from the point of the breastbone back to the pelvic bridge below the tail.   Make this cut through the abdominal wall with the knife-edge up, inserting the first two fingers into the incision to guide the knife from beneath and being infinitely careful not to cut the paunch or intestines. This done, cut around the anus and free it, tie it off with string, and draw it up into the body cavity. This should also include a doe's reproductive organs. A buck's sex organs can be easily removed while making the belly cut, but be sure of your hunting regulations. The law may require leaving the buck's scrotum in place.

Cut the diaphragm between chest and abdomen and reach far up into the chest cavity and sever the windpipe and esophagus. Some hunters split the chest to do this, freeing the ribs at their cartilage junctions with the breastbone. Other hunters, especially in cool weather, may never split the chest or remove its contents until they reach home.

The rectal area can also be removed by splitting the cartilaginous aitchbone of the deer's pelvis with a heavy knife or a belt ax, but be careful of this pelvic cut. If you're sloppy about it, you can ruin some prime "round."

After cutting out all anchoring membranes, the entire mass of viscera can be rolled out of the deer's carcass. Prop open the chest and abdomen with short sticks to permit rapid cooling. Many hunters never wash out a deer's body cavity, but prefer to wipe it out with clean rags or paper towels and permit a blood glaze to form.

But if the viscera have been cut while cleaning the deer, or if the deer was shot in the abdominal area, wash the body cavity thoroughly with clean water and flush out all blood and debris.

During the entire field-dressing process, do not allow meat to come in contact with hair, especially if the deer is a buck. Hair can taint the meat. Some hunters advocate immediate removal of the metatarsal glands on the hind legs. If this is done, wash your hands and knife thoroughly before getting on with the job. Removal of these glands is not necessary, however, if the deer is handled properly and care is taken to avoid rubbing the glands. The deer may be left unskinned. A deer carcass will cool readily with the hide attached, although larger game animals with heavier hides or thick coats may sour rapidly if skinning is delayed.

With the deer hog-dressed, it's ready to move to camp. If you're in good condition, in open country, and if the deer isn't large, you may choose to drape it over your shoulders in storybook fashion. But in any kind of poor light, timber, or brushland, this is a pretty fair way of getting scragged yourself. Few things are more dangerous than carrying a deer through hunting country, and it becomes work of the heaviest sort, for a freshly killed deer is as limp and boneless as a hundred-weight of gelatin.

There are patent devices for hauling deer, but most hunters prefer to drag them. This is easiest and best on snow, for dragging a deer over dry ground can bruise and soil the meat. But it may be the only choice.

Veteran guide and outdoorsman Joe Martin demonstrates the initial steps in field-dressing. The buck is a Texas whitetail taken by the editor.

In such a case, tie the forelegs together and lash the head to these legs with the muzzle pointing forward. The drag line is lashed to the forefeet, making a streamlined bundle that slips easily over most surfaces.

The most miserable two-man way of hauling a deer is by tying the feet over a long pole and carrying it with the carcass dangling and swinging freely. This can almost split a man to his wishbone when walking over rough ground. If you have a partner, bend the deer's forefeet around the back of its head, tie them in place, and lash a 4-foot pole to the antlers. With a man at each end of the short pole, the carcass can be easily dragged.

The single secret of sweet venison is to cool the meat as quickly as possible, and to keep it as cool as you can until it is processed.

CAMP CARE

If you plan to remain in camp for some time after the deer is shot, and if the law permits, it may be wise to skin and quarter the deer. The hide is split along the backs of the hind legs to the anus, pulled from the haunches and off the back, and worked off the thin-meated sides by pulling with one hand while hammering the taut hide away from the flesh with the butt of your fist. "Fisting" a hide is not difficult, and once the peeling has begun it may hardly be necessary to use your knife again until you come to the forelegs. If you plan to have the head mounted as a trophy, do not split the skin on the underside of the neck. Cut around the very base of the neck—perhaps even extending this cut around the foreshoulders and lower chest, and cut up the back of the neck to between the ears. Remove the head by cutting across the "Adam's apple" to the atlas joint— the only joint on the neck that has no interlocking bones.

When the deer is field-butchered, the quarters can be wrapped in muslin or cheesecloth to prevent magpies or Canada jays from attacking the meat as it hangs high in the tree. If the entire deer is to hang in camp for a few days, some hunters coat the exposed portions of meat with blood from the body cavity to form a "rind" or glaze that dries hard and seals the flesh from blowflies. On areas of heavy muscle that tend to stay moist and

On fairly open snow-covered terrain without obstacles or steep grades, a small deer like this Pennsylvania whitetail can be dragged easily after field-dressing. As the author mentions, however, the forelegs tend to hang up against brush, logs, fallen branches, rocks, and so on. Madson suggests that the drag line would work more smoothly if the deer's forelegs and head were lashed together, pointing forward. (Photo: U.S. Forest Service)

don't glaze, a coating of black pepper can be applied, and blowflies will avoid it. In addition to this, the entire body of the carcass may be cased in a tube of muslin.

Internal animal heat, rather than external weather heat, damages fresh deer meat quickest. Use spreader sticks to prop open the body cavity, and elevate the carcass in a tree so that it cools uniformly. If left on the ground, the meat in contact with the earth may cool so slowly that it spoils and this spoilage may extend to other areas. During the day in warm weather make every effort to keep the carcass in shade, hung in a place where air circulates freely around it.

If possible, start your trip home in early morning. After being in the chill night air, the carcass will be cool and in the best condition to travel. There's no longer much danger of ruining a deer by strapping it to a front fender next to the hot car engine; modern cars just aren't made that way. But if you carry the carcass in a car trunk or the back of the station wagon, be sure there are no gasoline cans or contaminants nearby. In cool weather the best place to carry the deer is on a cartop carrier where air can circulate evenly around it, or on a "duckboard" in the back of a pickup truck.

VENISON VIANDS

Prime deer meat, properly and promptly cared for, is delicious. People in the backcountry know this, and venison is one of their staples.

Then why will a city housewife condemn the "sour, gamey taste" of deer meat?

An old woodsman chooses his deer as carefully as the housewife buys a lamb roast. He doesn't want a trophy, but a fat young buck or, where it's legal, a plump young doe or yearling fawn. He shoots it near home, hog-dresses it in as little as 10 minutes, and has the deer cooled, skinned, and aging in the woodshed while a novice hunter is still stoning his knife. Result: properly handled venison, sweet and prime, and fresh liver and speckled gravy simmering on the range.

Assuming that the deer was in prime condition in the first place, the venison will be no better than the treatment it receives in the lapse between the bullet and butcher. No later processing can repair the damage done to venison in the early stages of cleaning and handling.

Once your deer is home, it should be aged before final butchering, packaging, and freezing. Many hunters allow the carcass to hang in a cool place or a walk-in refrigerator for about a week or 10 days. They leave the hide on to keep the meat from drying and turning dark. Butchering the deer is not a difficult job if you have the basic tools and a clean place to work. The butchering guides for calves and lambs—available from county extension agents—can also be used for deer. Most hunters, however, prefer to turn their deer over to commercial lockers for processing and freezing.

The great majority of these hunters have their deer processed into conventional chops, steaks, roasts, and burger. But a few people convert every scrap of deer meat to "chipped" venison, sausage, or other specialties.

My friend Bob Daubendiek is a big man with a big appetite, and his annual 150-pound supply of deer sausage never stretches from one deer season to the next. The first time I tumbled to Dauby's sausage was in a trout camp on Paint Creek when I rolled out of the sleeping bag to find a dozen scrambled eggs wearing a halo of golden-brown deer links. I can't recall how many trout we caught that day. But I'll never forget the smoky tang of Dauby's deer "sassige" just as the sun was touching the cedars on the ridge-crest, and the pileated woodpeckers were beginning their day's work on the wolf oaks back in Yellow River Forest. The dew forced us to wear hip boots to breakfast that morning. I ate about a pound of the sausages with my fingers and wiped my hands on my boots, and all morning my booted legs "chummed" trout in the long pools.

Dauby uses 50 pounds of pork with 50 pounds of venison, 4 ounces of "quick action pickle," and 2 pounds of pork sausage seasoning. He grinds the venison three times through the fine plate of a grinder, and grinds the pork once through a coarse plate. He mixes the ground meats with the pickle and seasoning and runs the entire batch once through a sausage plate. The ground and mixed sausage is then run into weiner-size casings and cold-smoked at under 100 degrees.

"The best bet," says Dauby, "is just to take your deer to most any locker plant and walk out a week later with an armload of clean, frozen, two-pound packages with twelve links of sausage in each."

He adds that the local locker plant is processing over 100 deer each year in this manner, and says: "These sausages are one reason why the womenfolk around these parts *send* their men deer hunting."

BUCKSKIN

It takes a heap of hunting to make a man a coat.

An average deerskin is good for about three or four pairs of gloves, but it takes at least three medium-size hides for a really good short jacket and as many as five hides if you want a real "Hickok tuxedo" that drips with tradition and 10-inch fringe.

In any case, your deerskin is worth investing some extra effort and money in. Buckskin is a remarkable leather, soft and immensely durable. But it does have drawbacks. When wet, it sops up water like a sponge and swiftly sags and stretches. Like the old Indian said: "Dry

All authorities agree that if a deer must remain in camp for some time, it should be hung well off the ground for cooling. There is some argument as to whether a head-up or head-down position is better. Elman points out in Appendix 3 that it's easier to hang a deer by the antlers, head-up, and that it will stay cool just as well in this position if spreader sticks are used to prop the body cavity open, as they should be. However, Madson notes that the deer should be skinned and quartered if you plan an extended stay in camp—and this can be a valid argument for the head-down position. A deer hung that way is easier to skin. In the kind of weather pictured here—with snow on the ground—prompt skinning isn't crucial, but it certainly is in hot weather. (Photo: Norm Nelson)

buckskin pants good for one man. Get'um wet, good for two men." And according to one frontiersman, buckskin moccasins "will wet through two days before it rains."

Historian Bernard De Voto wrote that many early Mountain Men preferred woolen trousers and hooded woolen "capotes" when they could get them, partly for the frontier snob appeal of such clothing but mostly because wet buckskin is clammy and stretchy, and dry buckskin is hot in warm weather. But by the time the fur brigades convened at the June "rondyvoo," they'd all be in buckskin again. The wool wore out swiftly; buckskin goes on forever.

Since the demise of ponyskin as a jacket leather, our softest and toughest leather is buckskin, which also makes up into fine vests, gloves, bags, and slippers. When my son was less than a year old, a friend made him a pair of tiny moccasins with fancy bead and threadwork on the vamps. And when Chris toddled down the main drag of Kenora, done up in his bright moccasins, plaid shirt, and galluses, he stopped every pulpcutter and Ojibwa who saw him.

If you have strong arms and a stronger stomach, you can tan your own buckskin. Don't try to leave the hair on, for hollow deer hair is brittle, easily broken, and won't wear well. But tanning is a smelly, tedious chore that you probably won't cotton to, and you'd be far better off sending your deerskins to a custom tanner.

Rub the skin side of your fresh deerhide with fine salt and spread it hairside down on a clean, dry surface. Brine will form. In a couple of days the hide should be folded skin to skin to keep it from becoming hard and dry.

Big tanneries seldom accept single skins. It's best to just send the deerskin to a taxidermist or someone specializing in trophy skins. He will probably mark it for identification and store it with other skins and hold it until he has a lot large enough to send to a tannery. However, there are a few commercial houses that specialize in buckskin and may tan your deerskin and make it up into any item you wish.

It will cost, but it's worth it. You'll own an item that's comfortable, durable, and uniquely personal. And when asked where you bought that handsome jacket you can snort: "Bought it? Man, I don't buy my clothes, I shoot 'em!"

Postscript on Bleeding, Caping, Home Taxidermy, and Other Details

by Robert Elman

In the very first chapter of this book, Dave Petzal predicted that there would be some minor disagreements among the contributors regarding such things as the best rifle action or load for hunting deer in a given region characterized by a particular type of terrain and cover. He was right, of course, and there were even minor differences of opinion about the "best" hunting method under given conditions. It's appropriate that this book should begin and end with such differences, because the varied opinions of experienced hunters add much to the fascination of deer hunting.

In the foregoing appendix, adapted from a publication issued by the Winchester-Western Conservation Department, John Madson tells—among other things—how to bleed your deer. He doesn't actually advise you to do it, so maybe we don't have a real difference of opinion. But he does say it may be necessary if the animal is hit in the head, neck, or spinal cord. I'm going way out on a limb by daring even to qualify any of John's statements, because he's one of the country's most knowledgeable and reliable experts in such matters. All the same, I'm in full agreement with only a third of John's advise as to when bleeding is necessary: A head-shot animal will very likely need draining by severing the carotid arteries or the jugular. In other cases—even when the shot is to the neck or spinal cord—bleeding is rarely necessary because the bullet wound itself initiates drainage, and this drainage continues as you go about field-dressing the game.

Several years ago I killed a good-size Texas mule deer with a neck shot. I was hunting with a guide, and he insisted that dressing it out was part of his job. In situations like that, I can be as slow about opening my knife as some people are about opening a wallet at a business lunch. I

A guide removes the metatarsal glands from the legs of a whitetail buck. Many experienced hunters insist on this procedure, but Madson and Elman agree that it isn't necessary—if you take care not to rub or cut the glands and thereby permit their secretion to taint the meat. (Photo: Robert Elman)

wondered if he'd bleed the animal. He didn't, and I wouldn't have, either, if he'd let me dress that deer. The lack of bleeding did not make the gutting job messier than it would otherwise have been, and the meat was delicious. There was a time when most hunters carried a sheath knife with a 6-inch blade. One of its uses was as a sticking knife. Nowadays more and more hunters carry a shorter (and therefore handier) sheath knife or a folding model such as I favor. If bleeding isn't necessary, neither is a 6-inch blade.

John also mentions the importance of preventing deer hair from getting on the meat. I agree, but only up to a point. Maybe I'm incurably sloppy, but I've never been able to dress and skin a deer without getting a little hair on the meat. I pick off what I notice, and before freezing the butchered cuts I blot away any more that I can find. But a few hairs invariably escape me, and they haven't yet soured a piece of my venison. I've asked several hunting acquaintances about their experiences in the matter. It turns out they're as sloppy as I am. However, that hair business may be more important in the warmer hunting regions.

I ought to add here that John and I are in complete agreement that it isn't necessary to cut away the knobby musk glands from the inner surface of a buck's hock joints, even if the animal is at the peak of the rut.   Another Texas guide I once hunted with—a superb hunter and all-round outdoorsman—thought I was out of my mind because I didn't want to bother slicing those glands off a whitetail I'd shot.   It was a case of his learning a "rule" during boyhood and ever afterward believing it as gospel.   If those glands aren't rubbed or cut while the deer is being dressed out, they won't taint the meat.

Before leaving the subject of myths that are hard to debunk, let me mention a more peculiar one.   In a couple of regions where I hunted quite some time ago, the local sportsmen insisted that when a deer was to be kept in camp for a while it had to be hung upside down.   Supposedly it would cool and age better that way.   Well, I can't see why that should be so.   In fact, if drainage hasn't quite stopped, an upside-down chest cavity must act as a catch basin, which doesn't seem at all desirable.   You don't

The editor collected this fine mule deer in south-central Texas.   A good shoulder mount was facilitated by proper—that is, generous—caping.   This is the first step in taxidermy and a crucial one, even though it may take place right in the field.   (Photo: Robert Elman)

need to spread the hind legs wide and hang the deer by them to keep the carcass cool; just keep the body opening wide, as John suggests, with spreader sticks. Besides, its much easier to hang a deer by its antlers.

In his section on camp care, John also has some good advice about preparing a trophy head for mounting. I'd just like to add a few details about this business of "caping," to use the traditional big-game hunter's expression. As he says, the right way (that is, the neat and easy way) to remove the head is to cut through the neck at the atlas joint—also known as the axial joint. If you do this, you won't need an ax or saw because you'll be able to remove the head simply by grasping it at the bases of the antlers and twisting it off. But this point is way up at the top of the neck (the first vertebra under the skull) and you don't want any cuts in the hide there; you have to take extreme care about parting the skin from the flesh and leaving enough skin for a generous wall mount. John's advice merits emphasis here: *Do not split the skin on the underside of the neck.* It also merits further elucidation:

Use a sharp, reasonably short knife. Holding it with the cutting edge up, use the point to slit the skin from the top of the withers straight up the back of the neck to the midpoint between the ears. Now, back at the withers, at the rear end of this cut, circle the body with another cut—down behind the shoulders and across the legs at the bottom of the bris-ket. The *bottom*. That will leave plenty of hide. You can then peel the skin forward, up to the ears and jaws, exposing the point where you want to cut through the neck. Finally, rub salt liberally into the flesh exposed under the head, and also into the flesh side of the cape—the hide you've left attached to the head. If you're going to have a taxidermist do the mounting, that's all there is to it except to freeze the head as soon as possible and keep it frozen until it goes to the taxidermist.

But many sportsmen these days are doing their own taxidermy, not just to save money (and mounting has become increasingly expensive) but because it's a fascinating hobby. A good home-mounted job will give you quite a sense of artistic accomplishment, and it isn't terribly difficult nor does it require very expensive and hard-to-find tools and materials. But on the other hand, nothing is more depressing than to botch a fine trophy. And if you do spoil it, the chances are that the damage can't be completely undone even by a professional taxidermist.

It's therefore an excellent idea not to make your first mounting attempt on a trophy that means a lot to you. Start by mounting a "learning" head—your next spike buck, for instance. It doesn't even have to be a deer. Any kind of game will help you learn the principles and tech-niques. Use a rabbit if you want to, or a coyote or a bobcat or anything you please. If you think this hobby might interest you, your first step must be to get a good book on the subject and follow its instructions carefully.   I can recommend Waddy F. McFall's book, *Taxidermy Step by Step* (Winchester Press, 1975).

A deer that really deserves mounting is apt to be large in body as well as antlers, and any hunter has a natural curiosity about the weight of his trophy buck.   Usually, in fact, a hunter is eager to know the weight of any deer he's taken, even a plump young spike or forkhorn.   However, it's not likely that you'll be able to weigh it before you get it out to a checkpoint, much less before you dress it out, so you'll have to be satisfied with a sensibly estimated live weight based on the weight of the hog-dressed carcass.   I've heard a lot of arithmetical formulas, some of them pretty complicated, but you just don't need any algebraic brainteasers to arrive at a close estimate.   I'll leave you with this last tip, which will make it easy for you to judge the weight of any deer you take: Forget the formulas and just remember the simple, imperfect but accurate enough rule that a deer's live weight is 25 percent more than its weight after you've field-dressed it.

Index

Index